Has The World Gone Completely Mad . . .?

Has the World Gone Completely Mad. . .?

Unpublished Letters to
The Daily Telegraph

EDITED BY
IAIN HOLLINGSHEAD

Aurum
Press

Quarto is the authority on a wide range of topics.

Quarto educates, entertains and enriches the lives of our readers—enthusiasts and lovers of hands-on living.

www.quartoknows.com

First published 2015 by
Aurum Press Ltd
74-77 White Lion Street
London N1 9PF
www.aurumpress.co.uk

A catalogue record for this book is available from the British Library.

ISBN 978 1 78131 517 0
Ebook ISBN 978 1 78131 547 7

10 9 8 7 6 5
2018 2017 2016

Typeset in MrsEaves by SX Composing DTP, Rayleigh, Essex
Printed and bound in Great Britain by
CPI Group (UK) Ltd, Croydon, CR0 4YY

SIR – While attending the cardiac clinic at Papworth Hospital today I ill-advisedly started to read your latest letters book, *What Will They Think of Next . . .?* Shortly thereafter I succumbed to uncontrollable laughter, much to the annoyance of my fellow patients, who were either waiting for – or had recently undergone – major heart surgery and were understandably in a sombre mood.

Fortunately, I was accompanied by my wife who was able to apologise to everyone on my behalf as I was unable to speak coherently.

My point, Sir, is that you should, in future editions, list places where reading your book is inappropriate, as this would avoid embarrassment to the reader and irritation to the public.

John Bebbington
Haslingfield, Cambridgeshire

SIR – The more I read the Letters page the more I realise just how much politicians are out of step with public opinion. Please can the editor double the space available as the contents are more interesting than most of the copy.

John Armstrong
Peacehaven, East Sussex

CONTENTS

INTRODUCTION

After seven years of writing introductions to these books I worried that I would run out of things to say. Fortunately, while words might fail me, they rarely leave our wonderful correspondents in the lurch. The world poses intractable problems; letter writers to *The Daily Telegraph* provide innovative solutions. How do we resolve the Greek crisis? Buy the Parthenon, move it to Hampstead Heath and get the Duke of Edinburgh to tell everyone to hurry the **** up. Who should present *Top Gear*? Miliband, Clegg and Farage – and certainly not Chris Evans, even if one of our male readers did once follow him into the ladies' loo in a hotel in East Yorkshire. Is Sepp Blatter a cad or a bounder? Even a cad wouldn't wear brown shoes with a dark suit. Where should London's next runway be built? Calais.

Admittedly, not all the world's dilemmas are so easily resolved, even by the combined wit and wisdom of our correspondents. How do you explain to your sister which team is actually 'winning' a cricket match? How will Ed Balls and Yvette Cooper manage on only one set of parliamentary expenses? What will David Cameron and George Osborne do with their beloved hi-vis Bob the Builder outfits now that they have won the election? There are, as

Donald Rumsfeld said, known knowns and known unknowns. Happily, whether showing a decisiveness or a curiosity all too rare in other walks of life, this year again finds the readers in fine fettle.

I am sometimes asked what makes a good *Telegraph* letter. Is it the Commodore in chapter seven, flanked, naturally, by a Colonel, wondering what happened to friendly beers after a rugby match? Or the pensioner in chapter eight reminiscing about his mocking Nazi salutes as a Bermondsey schoolboy during the Blitz? The disgruntled wife wondering whether the camera operator on Centre Court at Wimbledon is a man? Or M, our Bristol asset who believes himself to be the head of MI5, producing some torturous logic to 'prove' that Tony and Cherie Blair are in charge of ISIS? (M has shown admirable consistency in this regard; in *I Could Go On...* he accused Peter Mandelson of orchestrating an assassination in Dubai.)

The answer, of course, is that a good *Telegraph* letter is all of the above — and, above all, the combination of all of the above. The whole is more than the sum of the parts in this eclectic community of scribes, scholars and scoundrels. Our readers speak truth to power and powerful truths. I enjoy their company immeasurably.

It has certainly been a busy year for all letter-writers, whether resident at Clarence House, SW1, or Stratford-upon-Avon, Warwickshire (has it

replaced Tunbridge Wells as the 'Disgusted' centre of
dissent, wonders one correspondent?). Nick Clegg
and Ed Miliband were dispatched by the electorate
to spend more time with their hard-working families
and their kitchens. *Fifty Shades of Grey* returned
to the headlines, to the consternation of one
correspondent who still associates caning with the
pain of public school and another, a librarian, who
is reminded of her disappointment on first reading
Lady Chatterley's Lover. Meanwhile, it has been a bad year
for naturists, whether topless tourists arrested on
Mount Kinabalu (a surprise for our correspondent
who remembers the lovely local ladies of Batavia in
1945) or the topless ladies in the *Sun*.

2015 has also been a good year for anniversaries:
VE Day, which prompts a recollection of anarchy
in the ranks in Athens; Churchill's death, which
draws out a nurse who once took his temperature;
Waterloo and Magna Carta, which not even
our longest-serving readers are old enough to
remember – although one does suggest that now
would be an opportune moment to relieve the
government of its powers and place them back in the
hands of the monarch.

I shall spoil the jokes no more. Suffice to say,
you hold a bumper collection in your hands –
and, for that, I am immeasurably grateful, as ever,
to Christopher Howse, the Letters Editor; Sally
Peck, who mined the inbox once more with great

skill; Matt Pritchett; Cerys Hughes; Melissa Smith
at Aurum Press; and, of course, our unique and
brilliant correspondents. I like to imagine that when
the apocalypse comes, they will still find time to
dash off a quick letter or two to the Editor, perhaps
including a joke comparing the deadly asteroid to
the EU, a practical guide to making drinking water
out of radioactive puddles and a complaint that
the BBC bulletin heralding the end of the world
mispronounced the word *particularly*.

In the meantime, theirs is a welcome voice of
sanity in a world which often seems to have gone
completely mad.

Iain Hollingshead
London SE22

FAMILY LIFE AND TRIBULATIONS

HOT PANTS

SIR – In the heat of last summer I mentioned to a young lady friend that the pansies in her hanging basket would be suffering from dehydration if there was no rain while she was away on holiday.

The following week, with high temperatures and no rain, she emailed me from her holiday, finishing with the interesting line: 'Goodness knows what state my panties will be in after a week of this heatwave.'

I told her she should have taken a spare pair.

John Burney
Melbourne, Derbyshire

SIR – Buying a clematis plant recently, my wife and I were reminded that a friend's wife, who often organises charity coffee mornings for lady friends, had on one such occasion been addressed thus by the woman next-door:

'Oh, by the way, Thelma, will you ask David to trim your clitoris because it's growing over the top of the party wall?'

Is this a record?

M.C.M.
York

SIR – I was once unsteady from excessive sun in Turkey when the owner of a small taverna marched me to a chair and sat me down. He disappeared into his kitchen and returned with an onion, cut in half across the middle.

I had to bare my tummy and he rubbed it vigorously with the cut surface; it felt very cold and I was not fragrant thereafter. It did, however, work.

This is not a spoof.

Mary Crabtree
Tanworth-in-Arden, Warwickshire

SIR – One tip for staying cool in a heatwave is to avoid reading any column with a title like, 'Ten tips for staying cool in a heatwave'.

Robin Steggles
Holbrook, Suffolk

SIR – During the current heatwave we are being asked to make sure our elderly neighbours are coping with the situation. My wife asked who were our elderly neighbours.

After a pause I replied, 'We are.'

George Brown
Stretford, Lancashire

OAP MP

SIR – On our walk today my wife and I chatted with various retired neighbours and friends and set the

world to rights. As we neared home we both agreed
on the good use our Prime Minister could make of
this accumulated wisdom and wit, at little cost other
than occasional expenses.

Bill Davidson
Balderon, Nottinghamshire

SIR – If I took all the advice thrust at us in the
media about exercise, diet, smoking, drinking and
voting Conservative, could I accumulate it and live
forever, or can I limit my life by choosing only some
of the advice?

Dick Lawrie
March, Cambridgeshire

SIR – Now the BBC has been forced to fund free
television licences for the over-75s, will David
Cameron demand that travel companies fund free
travel for pensioners?

Richard Francis
Norwich, Norfolk

SIR – I fail to see why so much fuss is made of the
three old-aged pensioners supposedly involved
with the Hatton Garden heist? Have we not
been encouraged to find a hobby upon entering
retirement?

Charles Holcombe
Brighton, East Sussex

SIR – If they are sentenced to an English prison, what a wonderful, well-equipped environment in which to live during one's dotage – especially compared to a National Health nursing home.

Martin Thurston
Liphook, Hampshire

SIR – My elderly person's bus pass has the instruction alongside my photo: 'Expiry Date 01 June 2015'. Ho hum.

Michael Johnson
Woolavington, Somerset

SIR – While I was walking down the High Street in black leather trousers a young Italian in a white van was sitting in the passenger seat, window down, smoking a cigarette.

'Sexy Mama!' he cried.

I grinned all week. I am 66.

Linda Major
London SW15

FIFTY SHADES OF SLUDGE

SIR – Christmas approaches, together with the start of my seventh decade. My trepidation is the prospect that all future clothing presents will be in fawn, camel, almond, beige and, of course, taupe. Why is

it that advancing years brings the expectation that
you will delight in being dressed in varying degrees
of sludge?

A.L.
Chelmsford, Essex

SIR – For me it is tantamount to a tragedy when
an old but comfortable shoe starts to let water in
through the sole. A friend of mine assured me that
he enjoyed months of extra wear by lining his with
folded solicitors' letters.

He reckoned that lawyers' letters alone would
suffice as only they could afford the best quality paper.

In these paperless times a sheet of copier paper
would not be the same. Then again, you could still
get some satisfaction in imagining with every damp
step taken that your foot was on your lawyer's throat.

B. Maskell
Croyde, Devon

SIR – The love affair with culottes and jumpsuits
continues, as shown on your fashion pages today.

More than 20 years ago my husband bought
me a culottes-style dress while in Madrid. It was
beautiful, split-legged and buttoned up the front.

However, when there is a need for a trip to the
loo, how is this achieved without a strip-down,
followed by an inelegant attempt to hold the
garment between one's knees? I will say no more.

I cannot be alone in making this discovery. Maybe the items are designed by men?

Gaynor Tunbridge
North Cheriton, Somerset

IM ON THE TOILT

SIR – I had necessity to venture to the Gents last night while watching the football and already present at one of the urinals was a youth of the younger generation. As I lined up and undertook the required task, he continued to text.

Have we really produced a generation who cannot be without their mobile devices for a single second? It is truly baffling.

Jeff Stanners
Kenilworth, Warwickshire

SIR – Mobile phones should only be used in the pub for photographing empty glasses and texting the picture to the bloke smoking outside who is due to buy the next beer.

Philip Saunders
Ditchingham Dam, Suffolk

SIR – Your article 'Putting on weight? Check the size of your wine glass' left me wondering. I am losing weight: do I need a much larger glass? I am obviously burning too many calories on my refill trips.

Terry Ashton
Oakhill, Somerset

SIR – I recently visited a pub in Wimbledon and received absolutely no change out of a £20 note for four drinks. The pub was heaving, with at least four football matches broadcast at the same time.

This is not a pub. A pub is like the place I visited recently in Elstead in Surrey where it took 25 minutes to get a pint because the barrel had just run out and the landlord (apparently a former Italian league footballer) had absolutely no idea what he was doing.

John Hutton
East Molesey, Surrey

SIR – My main gripe with pubs is staff deliberately clashing empty bottles into bins so as to make customers jump.

Colin Laverick
London WC2

SIR – In the last 12 months I have made a rule that while conversing with someone, I would go silent if he or she uttered the words 'Yeah, yeah, yeah…' or started tapping a smartphone.

There have been an awful lot of silences; some, but not all, noticed by the other party.

For the record, I'm 50, a father of teenagers, interesting, handsome and modest.

L.R. Smith
Haywards Heath, West Sussex

THE BIRDS, THE BEES AND THE KNEES

SIR – Tristram Hunt is suggesting sex lessons for five-year-olds. Can I assume that in the future, when a father sits his son on his knee and says, 'Let's have a talk about the Birds and the Bees', the answer will be, 'What do you want to know, Dad?'

May Heaven help us.

Doug Humphreys
South Petherton, Somerset

SIR – I cannot tell if Gwyneth Paltrow's latest fad, steaming her vagina, is intended to keep it warm, keep it clean or get the creases out.

Kevin Platt
Walsall, West Midlands

THINGS THAT GO BUMP IN THE NIGHT

SIR – Rowan Pelling's article triggered an old
memory. In the late 1950s, in the early years
of our marriage, we spent a blissful eight days
in Paris. Our hotel was cheap but clean and the
partition walls between the bedrooms were rather
flimsy.

At the end of our first day, we had just settled
into bed with a glass of wine apiece when our
bedstead started to shake rhythmically. As the speed
and volume increased we hastily parked our wine in
a safer place.

Joanna Wiesner
Bath, Somerset

SIR – On holiday in Madeira a few years ago my
wife and I were bemused by the wailings of one of
our neighbouring guests in the hotel. The following
morning we thought we would be able to spot the
offender at breakfast. Of course, everyone else was
playing the same game.

Keith Macpherson
Houston, Renfrewshire

SIR – Among the many names such as 'the old
trout', 'GHQ' and 'she who'll be obeyed at all
times', my favourite, when introducing my wife to

new acquaintances, is, 'the light of my life and the heartthrob of my bedsprings'.

Paul Harrison
Organford, Dorset

WOLF-WHISTLE WHILE YOU WORK

SIR – Your front-page story on the criminalisation of wolf-whistles took me back several years.

A colleague had a rather plain wife who was known for a short temper. One day she passed a group of men who were digging a roadside hole. A sudden wolf-whistle made her turn round and march purposefully toward the men, a Gorgon-like expression on her face.

She demanded to know which of them had whistled. Eventually one young man looked up sheepishly and said it was him.

Her scowl turned to a smile as she said: 'Thank you, that's the nicest thing that's happened to me for ages.'

E.F.
Edinburgh

SIR – When on the receiving end of wolf-whistles, my friends and I used to remark disparagingly that men would whistle at anything in a skirt.

It seems as if political correctness, the law or general respect for women has taken over because I am no longer whistled at, despite still wearing a skirt.

Or maybe it's because I'm 76 and walk with a stick.

Valerie Currie
Brockworth, Gloucestershire

SIR – Why have worksite wolf-whistles been replaced by extra loud belching, especially in corridors and any space likely to produce a good echo? A wolf-whistle had its place – at least one would know when there was a lady about.

Joseph G. Dawson
Withnell, Cheshire

SIR – Soon the way to prove that a woman has given sexual consent will no doubt require the use of cameras, unless a form has been satisfactorily completed beforehand in quadruplicate.

This will make the whole issue black and white (or coloured if you prefer). However, it will require that the conduct of such matters may only take place in the bedroom. So very Victorian. Individuals with more exotic tastes will need to have more extensive camera coverage.

Our parents and grandparents who fought two

world wars for our freedom would be horrified beyond measure how we have silently allowed state control to creep into our every action.

It is but one step away that, like dogs, we shall be required to be chipped.

John Nickell-Lean
Southwold, Suffolk

POOP SCOOP SLEUTH

SIR – You have recently published letters on this subject and, although a little late, I thought you might be amused by this story.

One day I took my St. Bernard for a walk along the Dover sea front and he unfortunately added to the considerable mess that was already there. To my embarrassment I found I had forgotten to bring the appropriate plastic bag, so I hurried back to my car and drove him home.

I felt so guilty about this that I armed myself with the necessary accoutrements and returned to the sea front until I found the prize specimen worthy of a St. Bernard.

I told my wife who thought it so funny that she told all her friends. I couldn't see the joke until my wife explained that she didn't want to be associated with a crackpot who might be seen walking around without a dog looking for the best specimens to take home.

Dr R.J. Thompson
Guston, Kent

THE SECOND COMING

SIR – Some years ago I lived next door to a young couple who kept the wife's horse in a stable at the bottom of the garden. Eventually a stray cat gave birth there to one kitten, which she decided to keep.

'I'm going to call it Jesus because it was born in a stable,' she told me.

She changed her mind when I pointed out to her the inadvisability of standing at the door late at night shouting: 'Jesus! Jesus!'

Rosalind Hellewell
Scunthorpe, Lincolnshire

SIR – As many of your readers will know, the starling is a great mimic. Years ago I stayed in a pub in Somerset and was awoken at 5a.m. by the electronic sounds of the bar's fruit machine, only to discover that it was actually a beautiful starling singing away on the gutter outside my bedroom window. I was enthralled.

The blackbird is also capable of the same trick.

For the last three years my wife and I have been
entertained by a blackbird which includes in
its glorious repertoire a perfect rendition of the
whistle my wife uses to call her dog. This can
lead to some confusion, however, as this is
the same whistle my wife uses to summon me to
the house.

Paul Sargeantson
Britwell Salome, Oxfordshire

ENDURING LOVE

SIR – I have had to smile at the recent letters about
Valentine Cards. I have sent my husband the same
card each year (originally as a joke) since 1963. Each
year it gets a new envelope. The deceit has not as yet
been noticed, so I must have saved lots of money in
the process.

Paula Willcock
Castle Cary, Somerset

SIR – I am reminded of the occasion of my mother's
birthday. Having forgotten all about it until that
morning, my stepfather dashed to the corner store
without his spectacles, chose a pretty card, wrote a
loving message and proudly handed it to my mother
at breakfast.

She was at a loss to know how to interpret the

sentiments of the card, which blithely wished her 'Bon Voyage'.

Margaret Weare
Stone, Kent

SIR – When ordering a cake for my mother's 70th birthday from a smart Marylebone patisserie, I was given an album from which to choose and requested the splendid cream and fresh fruit gateaux with 'Happy Birthday' on top, instead of 'Happy Birthday you big fat b*****d'.

I have often wondered why the shop featured that version in its album.

Sue Keane
Henley-on-Thames, Oxfordshire

SIR – My husband, who enjoys the art of conversation, received a card from me on his birthday.

Husband, in full hiking gear and backpack: 'I've joined the Ramblers.'

Wife, back turned to him: 'Walking or talking?'

The house was strangely silent for the rest of the day.

Lesley Thompson
Lavenham, Suffolk

TILL DEATH DO US START

SIR – My wife and I have 184 years between us and have been married for 74 years.

In 1941 I was given a week's leave from the army. Determined to propose, I sought out my girlfriend at her reserved occupation at an undertakers. I was invited into the Chapel of Rest and asked whether I would like to sit on elm or oak.

I chose the (empty) oak coffin – and I was accepted.

R.S. Eades
Maidenhead, Berkshire

SIR – My husband proposed to me from the depths of his sick bed, where I was nursing him on night duty in Benghazi. I spent the rest of the night wondering if I had heard him correctly or if maybe he was hallucinating. We are still together 53 years later.

Mary L. Crooke
Liverpool

SIR – My wife, Joan, gave me a silk stocking during the Second World War. I wore it round my neck on every one of the 36 bombing missions I flew as a Bomb Aimer in Lancasters of 44 (Rhodesia) Squadron, 5 Group, Bomber Command.

Joan and I married after my fourth operational

mission, not knowing what lay ahead. However, we knew the full meaning of the words that Alice Duer Miller wrote: 'But lovers in war-time, Better understand, The fullness of living, With death close at hand'.

We had a wonderful 55 years of marriage. Joan died in 1999, but the silk stocking is still where she put it in my log book after I had completed my operational tour.

Bill Spence
Ampleforth, North Yorkshire

SIR – My wife and I met over the sample bottles in a hospital pathology laboratory in 1960. Shortly after our relationship became general knowledge, I was summoned to the Chief Technician's office. He wanted to reassure himself that my intentions were honourable.

This paternal attitude to female laboratory staff may be out of date today, but suffice to say we celebrate our Golden Wedding later this year.

Ian Wiseman
Ivybridge, Devon

NATIONAL WAITROSE SERVICE

SIR – Having witnessed nurses enjoying a break while a patient desperately pressing her bell for help was being ignored, I cannot but compare this with the care and attention lavished on my wife and me while we had lunch in our local Waitrose.

Perhaps trainee nurses should be required to attend a supermarket staff-training course before being allowed to attend to their 'clients' on the hospital wards.

Paul Corser
Selborne, Hampshire

SIR – If any of your readers belong to the group of shoppers who perform a u-turn at the tills and pull the trolley through the check-out, perhaps they could explain the advantages of this manoeuvring. I haven't been able to fathom any – although the entertainment value of watching their antics is undeniably high.

Frederick Reuben Parr
Tyldesley, Lancashire

SIR – Looking around our kitchen table post shopping today my wife pointed out the lesson in geography. Among the many delights were: bananas from Columbia, HP Sauce from the Netherlands, apples from France, biscuits from Spain, pears from Belgium and, from England, a big bag of Uncle Joe's Mint Balls for me.

Joseph G. Dawson
Withnell, Lancashire

SIR – 47 pips in a yellow grapefruit! Is this
a record or did it have a one-night stand with a
melon?

Gerry Draper
Watford, Hertfordshire

AS FAT AS A LORD

SIR – Your headline 'Peers, not parents, drive
teenage obesity' intrigued me until I realised that it
was not members of the House of Lords who were
being blamed. Given the weight of some of them,
however, perhaps it was an understandable mistake
to make.

Robin Bryer
Closworth, Somerset

SIR – How do all these obese people actually
manage to eat so much? In our late, very active
fifties, neither my wife nor I can manage to
overeat without dyspepsia and the feeling of
being a beached whale.

Adrian Waller
Woodsetts, South Yorkshire

SIR – The obese are simply slim people in disguise.
We are all insane. Gluttony, narcissism, swearing,
laziness, telling lies, committing adultery, leching,

racism, violence. The list of human imperfections is a long and varied one.

Tom Venour
Hampton, Middlesex

SIR – My wife was travelling recently on a packed train from Wolverhampton to Telford. When the guard got off at one station he was unable to re-board despite his requests to 'Move down the carriage, please.'

My wife called out: 'Would all the slim people stand up, and all the plump people sit down, please.'

There was some laughter but they did as they were bid.

Peter Sichel
Wellington, Shropshire

HOW TO AVOID A TUBE STRIKE

SIR – Happily, I avoided this week's tube strike, which evidently caused mass frustration and anger for many.

I achieved this by living in County Durham, some 250 miles north of the capital, where houses can still be purchased at a reasonable sum, the people are almost universally friendly and a pint of good beer will set one back less than £2.

I expect I am far from the only one wondering

why Londoners put up with so much hassle for such meagre returns — especially as many will earn less than a tube driver.

Is it only the larger number of Tinder members in the capital that keeps so many of them on the human treadmill of ever-diminishing returns?

Dr Gregory Carter
Durham

DUTCH CYCLING COURAGE

SIR – Your correspondent compares the Dutch cycling style with that of Britain. During numerous business trips to Copenhagen I have noticed how most Danish cyclists ride old-fashioned, sit-up-straight bicycles and wear normal everyday clothing.

In Britain, however, most cyclists look as though they are taking part in a race. I wonder if that frame of mind is contributing to the number of accidents which occur here.

Roger Merryweather
Whiteshill, Gloucestershire

SIR – What utter tosh: Dutch cyclists are just as bad or worse. I have nearly been hit twice by cyclists in the last 24 hours: one on the pavement, the other on a crossing.

From now on, if possible, my walking stick will be going through their front wheels.

Michael Peel
Hampton Hill, Middlesex

PUMP ACTION

SIR – You report the case of a pilot who taxied a 747 the wrong way down a runway due to poor eyesight.

Some years ago my brother was a pillion passenger on a motorbike driven by a fellow officer on their submarine. They were on their way for a 'Run ashore' in London. Suddenly, the driver started waving frantically, then turned to my brother and said, 'I am losing my appeal, those girls didn't wave back.'

My brother looked back and realised that the two girls were in fact BP petrol pumps. His immediate concern wasn't that the man in front of him was in charge of the day-to-day running of one of Her Majesty's submarines, but that they had some way to go to get to London, and then he had the return journey to look forward to after a night out.

Paul Rutherford
Bishops Sutton, Hampshire

CRUFTS' DOG'S DINNER

SIR – I was disgusted to read reports of a dog at
Crufts being given poison-laced meat. I dearly hope
the culprit is found, if only to learn his technique,
since I can't even get my dog to take his worming
tablets, however I conceal them.

Ian Eyres
Llanyblodwel, Shropshire

SIR – Skulldoggery at Crufts?

Steven Barrington
Antrobus, Cheshire

SIR – There is no excuse for poisoning at Crufts.
The dogs have done nothing to deserve such a
terrible fate.

The practice could, however, be introduced for
the BAFTAs and Oscar ceremonies to liven up the
events.

Arthur W.J.G. Ord-Hume
Guildford, Surrey

CHOICE WORDS

SIR – It was with some surprise that I read that
Tim Bevan, whose letter you published yesterday,

was disgusted with Stephen Fry's choice of words during the BAFTA Awards.

Having known Mr Bevan for some time, I can attest to his voracious and at times vivid command of the English language. I dare say he could expand even Mr Fry's prodigious vocabulary. He has certainly expanded mine.

Oliver Bevan (Tim Bevan's nephew)
London SE22

SIR – God may have the characteristics attributed to Him by Stephen Fry, but He is nowhere near as obnoxious as Fry, nor, it seems, as oft quoted.

Frank Felton
Stapleford, Cambridgeshire

SIR – Do you think it likely that at some time in the distant future, we might have an awards ceremony in this country that does not feature Stephen Fry as a presenter?

Stuart Roberts
Southport, Merseyside

SIR – Life imitates art. Following the Brit awards, at last we have a real Fallen Madonna with the Big Boobies.

E.K. Griffith
London E11

ANTI-SOCIAL
MEDIA

HORRIBLE HISTORIES

SIR – I think it is time for an on-screen indicator during programmes such as *Wolf Hall*. I am quite fed up with having to fact-check elements of an historical drama when recollections from my rather distant history syllabus beg to differ.

I propose a yellow card to indicate information that is disputed, conjecture or a modified truth; and a red card to indicate entirely fictional information. The viewer can then spend less of their viewing time buried in history books or the internet.

Of course, programme makers could always stick to historical accuracy, but I suppose that is too much to ask.

P.J. Bryant
Wisbech, Cambridgeshire

SIR – I'm not bothered by the authenticity of film and television drama because I avoid watching if possible, although others in the house do.

What I find more frustrating is that the same faces crop up so frequently. How can you take Chief Inspector So-and-So seriously today when he was the villain yesterday? I much prefer my drama in a good book; in my mind's eye the characters are unique and believable.

That said, I'm quite enjoying *Wolf Hall*, except

when King Henry appears and I see Captain Winters from Band of Brothers.

Roger Wood
Leintwardine, Shropshire

SIR — Does anybody agree with me that Mark Rylance may have loosely based his Cromwell on Eeyore?

Matthew Scott
Henley-on-Thames, Oxfordshire

SIR — If the actors in *Wolf Hall* are allowed to use the phrase 'That's for sure', as they did in tonight's episode, can they also be equipped with LED torches rather than candles, so that we can all see what is going on?

John Wilson
Princes Risborough, Buckinghamshire

SIR — Hilary Mantel is not alone in trying to make the subject matter of an historical novel topical to the present day. I do, however, struggle with her claim that the Tudors' abiding fascination for modern readers arises from them being 'just like us'.

None of us face the dynastic realpolitik that dominated their lives. Nor did the Tudors wrestle with career break decisions before having children.

'They leap out of the history books,' she writes. 'You find them next to you in the street.'

Tudor doppelgangers may be on Hilary's streets, but I'm relieved to say there aren't many here in Ramsbottom.

Andrew Todd
Ramsbottom, Lancashire

SIR – Your report that the second episode of *Wolf Hall* lost about one million viewers to *Midsomer Murders* may be taken as an inference regarding their respective qualities. In response I would respectfully point out that the *Sun* has the largest newspaper circulation.

Arthur Bayley
Tyldesley, Lancashire

RED-TOP HAMPERS

SIR – What awful news that the *Sun* is to no longer print pictures of nubile young ladies displaying their 'top hamper'.

This adult comic will no longer be attractive to leering old louches and slobbering inadequates, like me.

Sid Davies
Bramhall, Cheshire

SIR – News that the *Sun* is to abandon carrying topless, Page 3 photographs is enough to depress any red-blooded man. I only hope that they will not do the same thing with my Braille copy.

Andrew H.N. Gray
Edinburgh

SIR — 'Je Suis Page 3.' Morning tea breaks throughout the land will be duller with its passing.

Mike Denby
Addingham, West Yorkshire

SIR — I am minded of Lord Macaulay's remark: 'The Puritans hated bear-baiting, not because it gave pain to the bear, but because it gave pleasure to the spectators.'

Paul Donert
West Wickham, Cambridgeshire

SIR — If Page 3 was degrading to women, why was the famous WI calendar not considered in like manner?

Anne F. Bloor
Burton Overy, Leicestershire

SIR — Now that the *Sun* has dropped Page 3, is there any chance that the *Telegraph* will drop *Downton*?

Adrian Lloyd-Edwards
Stoke Fleming, Devon

SIR — An undertaking by the *Telegraph* of a daily picture of Sam Cam, Pippa Middleton, Joan Bakewell,

Lady Archer or Felicity Kendal would gladden the hearts of many of us.

Dr Bertie Dockerill
Shildon, County Durham

POLDARK PRUDES, PERVS AND PEDANTS

SIR – Will you please refrain from publishing any more photographs of that *Poldark* bloke. I can cope with seeing his naked torso every day, but my wife is suffering from the vapours.

David Nesbitt
Irthlingborough, Northamptonshire

SIR – Perhaps the *Poldark* actor Aidan Turner, whose scything skills have been criticised, should have first practised on his abundant chest hair, which the *Telegraph* insists upon showing to readers on a regular basis.

Ted Shorter
Hildenborough, Kent

SIR – Can someone explain why it is acceptable for women to admire physical male beauty in a way that is totally unacceptable the other way round? We even had Zoe Ball giving Aidan Turner an imaginary kiss on her Monday radio programme, having already spent a good 20 minutes on the subject of Poldark's rippling torso before her osculation.

I am quite sure that if dear old Ken Bruce, for whom Ms Ball was standing in, drooled over Demelza in a similar way, the feminist outrage would have been volcanic.

It's all very puzzling.

D.K. Mason
Harrogate, North Yorkshire

SIR – Men of Britain, you may finally relax now Poldark has been dragged off to Truro jail. Over the past few weeks, in an attempt to win back my wife, I have tried the unshaven look, the tousled hair look (not so effective in grey) and long moody looks, all to no avail.

Drinking wine at breakfast certainly caught her attention, though.

When is *Downton* back on?

Philip Armstrong
Windmill Hill, East Sussex

SIR – Unlike many viewers, while Poldark was disrobing, I was looking at the sunrise. I was astonished to see that this scene must have been shot in the Antipodes (or at least the southern hemisphere) as the sun was seen moving north after appearing above the horizon.

Long way to go for one scene — I would have thought Cornwall could occasionally supply a sunrise.

Keith Rogers
Alresford, Hampshire

SIR — Why does it take Poldark's horse so long to gallop between his new and former homes, when his wife just casually strolls between them in no time at all? Surely it is not another Cornish satnav problem?

Brian Christley
Abergele, Conwy

SIR — On returning from a four-day sojourn to Cornwall I would like to take the opportunity to congratulate the producers of *Poldark* for managing to find a piece of land that was not covered with wind turbines or solar panels.

Willy Pledger
Selsey, West Sussex

SIR — In his piece about howlers in *Poldark* Michael Deacon omitted the most egregious of all: someone reading from the marriage service managed to say 'Wilt thou hast . . .?'

The BBC had managed to assemble a scriptwriter, a director, a producer and an actor who, between them, had no knowledge of grammar or modern

German and had not read the Book of Common Prayer. Where do they find these people?

Philip Roe
St Albans, Hertfordshire

SIR — I wonder if the BBC realises that Poldark is an anagram of 'old krap'?

A.S.
Aspley Guise, Bedfordshire

SIR — I am sorry that no one takes snuff in *Poldark*. There are three advantages for the snuff taker: you cannot catch a cold; you may take it in church — by leave of Pope Benedict XIII in 1725; and you may take it in hospital. I propose to snuff it on my last sneeze.

Quentin de la Bedoyere
London SW19

JUST A MINUTE, TENNANT

SIR — I cannot see why David Tennant is earning so many plaudits for speaking for a minute without hesitation, deviation or repetition on the radio panel game show *Just A Minute*. Rather than appearing in game shows he should be putting all his efforts into solving the Sandbrook case in *Broadchurch*, thereby putting us all out of our misery.

John Hayles
Southend-on-Sea, Essex

SIR – If his role in *Broadchurch* is anything to go by, David Tennant's monologue on *Just A Minute* wasn't interrupted because nobody could understand what he was saying.

Madeline Glancy
Prestwich, Lancashire

SIR – The actors in *Broadchurch* should forget about trying to adopt a Dorset accent. No one around here speaks like that. It comes across more like a mixture of Welsh and Irish.

Ron Kirby
Dorchester, Dorset

SIR – Since I have been retired I have observed that my wife watches factual murder programmes. Should I be concerned?

George Brown
Manchester

GARDEN OF HADES

SIR – We are well into spring and the Chelsea

Flower Show looms nigh. Soon the BBC will abandon its cooking programmes and replace them with gardening ones. We will witness hugely enthusiastic presenters, mostly men, who can tell the difference between weeds and flowers, are skilled at propagating and pruning, and can turn over five cubic metres of loamy soil with one thrust of the spade without breaking into a sweat or swearing.

To hell with them all!

Malcolm Allen
Berkhamsted, Hertfordshire

SIR — Having watched programmes showing what are described as Chelsea gardens on television this week, I wonder why such structures, with incorporated buildings, flowing water and even 200 tons of Chatsworth rocks can be so described.

While washing up after dinner I looked into my garden comprising herbs, flower beds, soft fruits, trees in flower, beds of seasonal native flowers, climbing roses, lawns, a bird bath, a weather vane, a barbecue, table and chairs and, of course, my dog.

My partner's comment was: 'Now, that's what I call a garden.'

Peter Platt-Higgins
Mere, Wiltshire

SIR — Having just bought a pack of soft lavatory rolls I read the blurb on the back and noticed the diminishing number of sheets on each roll – not that you would know it from looking at the diameter of the roll. They increase the diameter of the cardboard tube in the middle, thus masking the trick.

I am aware of this because my wife uses the tubes as root trainers for her vegetable plants. They are excellent, as they rot away having done their job and cost nothing.

D.A.
Cley, Norfolk

INDIAN SUMMERS' VICES

SIR – I'm very much enjoying *Indian Summers* but just one thing is niggling me. Has anyone else noticed the fake wisteria draping Chotipool, the residence of the Viceroy's private secretary? It has been in full flower week after week. I'm expecting the 'blooms' to make it to the end of the series.

James Logan
Portstewart, County Londonderry

SIR – Having been born in Ceylon and worked there for many years I am fascinated by the history of the Raj in neighbouring India, so I was looking forward to watching *Indian Summers*. It was so awful and full of clichés that we switched off before the end of the first episode. The only good bits were the Indian scenery and bird calls – always so nostalgic.

David Perkins
Wimborne, Dorset

NOW, THAT'S NOT WHAT I CALL MUSIC

SIR – Is the BBC deliberately tormenting us? Is there, somewhere, a whole Department for Awful Signature Tunes?

The music that opens Radio 4's otherwise enjoyable *The Unbelievable Truth* sounds to me like a guitar player with hiccups bouncing down a set of stairs.

The intro to the much-esteemed *Reunion*, with the wonderful Sue MacGregor, would – to my mind – be better suited to a group of bored mourners in widows' weeds and black suits sitting round an open coffin, curtains closed.

As for the *Now Show*, if you lived next door you'd apply for a Noise Abatement Order.

Can we not just have some nice sing-along tunes to start them off? Like the *Archers*, perhaps?

Chris Hampson
Ashley Green, Buckinghamshire

SIR – The popularity of *All Aboard! The Canal Trip* demonstrates that all that silly music which producers use in documentaries is entirely unnecessary. It merely obscures the dialogue.

F.G. Sheard
High Hurstwood, East Sussex

EASTENDING IT ALL

SIR – To be fair to my partner, who cheerfully endures the odd televised football match, I have stopped marching out of the room at the first dreaded drumbeat of the *EastEnders* theme tune and try to immerse myself in the crossword.

This week, however, has plumbed new depths. I honestly believe that a warning should be broadcast before each episode along the lines of, 'If you are suffering from suicidal tendencies, this programme may well tip you over the edge'.

Stuart Smith
Houghton, Cambridgeshire

SIR – I feel I must agree with Diane Coyle, the vice-chairman of the BBC Trust, when she says that '*EastEnders* is too white'. This was one of the reasons I stopped watching *Star Trek*; I felt there should have been more Klingons and Romulans.

Stephen Roberts
Catcott, Somerset

people. Some viewers like to watch old men in jeans trying to be 21 again.

David Hall
Banstead, Surrey

SIR – Isn't it only 14 years ago that the then Deputy Prime Minister, Jeremy Prescott, punched a protester in North Wales? Far from being sacked he remained in post and has gone on to sit in the House of Lords as Baron Prescott.

Perhaps Clarkson should be sent to the House of Lords as Baron Clarkson of Brands Hatch.

Lieutenant Colonel Richard King-Evans
Hambye, Normandy, France

SIR – With popular support for Mr Clarkson standing at around 1 million 'votes' how many MPs could he replace?

Dean Alders
Camberley, Surrey

SIR – Now that we know that all three presenters are leaving *Top Gear*, this gives the BBC an opportunity to reformat the show to suit their politics. I suggest Ed Miliband as the lead with John Bercow and Natalie Bennett supporting.

We could have exciting features such as 'The Star in the Politically Correct Car', where contestants have to see how far they can go in a battery car, or

'Land's End to John O'Groats in 20 recharges'.

Since these presenters do not seem to me to be red-meat eaters there will also be no possibility of another fracas.

Such a format is bound to be a winner.

Dave Cruickshank
Knowle, West Midlands

SIR – As political leaning is more important to the BBC than behaviour, how about Russell Brand as the new *Top Gear* presenter?

Tony Manning
Barton on Sea, Hampshire

SIR – Since Kate Moss has got herself into trouble on an easyJet flight by having a meltdown over her foodstuff of choice being unavailable, she has presumably disqualified herself from being the next presenter of *Top Gear*.

That's one, at least.

Richard Light
Hitchin, Hertfordshire

SIR – I'm surprised the BBC haven't yet asked Fiona Bruce to present *Top Gear*. She seems to present everything else.

J. Newton-Lewis
Chichester, West Sussex

SIR – Jeremy Paxman would be tremendous on *Top Gear* and Jeremy Clarkson would be even more fearful on *Newsnight*.

Michael East
London N1

SIR – Enough is enough, I say. Are all Jeremys predisposed to be rude, arrogant and impatient? Jeremy Clarkson, Jeremy Vine, Jeremy Paxman – spot the difference.

Sarah Drew
Tillingham, Essex

SIR – I guess if Clarkson returned to *Top Gear* as Stig, no one would be any the wiser.

David Laycock
Castlemorton, Worcestershire

SIR – Am I alone in thinking that Radio 2 used to be a very pleasant music programme to be awoken by, until Chris Evans became the host? His shouting and bawling nonsense chat will be well suited to taking over *Top Gear*.

Michael Scott
Welbury, North Yorkshire

SIR – I once met Chris Evans after following him into the Ladies at the Bell Hotel in Driffield. I wanted to talk to him but he explained he wanted to get away from the reporters and cameras to have a pee in peace. I left him to get on with his business.

Terry Duncan
Bridlington, East Yorkshire

FIFTY SHADES AND I

SIR – At breakfast this morning a radio programme informed us that *Fifty Shades of Grey* is due to be released this week.

My wife said that she thought it would flop. I made no reply and gazed out of the window.

Rod Morris
Rodney Stoke, Cheshire

SIR – My wife tells me that the new film *Fifty Shades of Grey* is to be in colour. Am I missing something?

Simon Eagle
Walkington, East Yorkshire

SIR – Forget *Fifty Shades*. I am waiting for the film of Dominique Strauss-Kahn's memoirs.

Rowland Aarons
London N3

SIR – Regarding Dominique Strauss-Kahn's court case, if anybody is struggling with a definition for the word *oxymoron,* I think 'classy sex party' might do it.

Phil Warner
Alvechurch, Worcestershire

SIR – I am reminded of an intriguing advertisement which I assumed to be a misspelling, but which, in these times of works such as *Fifty Shades of Grey*, left me not wholly certain on the matter. It was an advertisement for bridal leather.

Graeme W.I. Davidson
Edinburgh

SIR – Fifty Shades of Purple?
Rose's is red,
Violet's is blue.
Would you like me to cane
Your bottom for you?

James Bacon
Atch Lench, Worcestershire

SIR – As the inmate of a minor public school in the 1960s the swish and thwack of cane on young flesh was the mood music of my youth.

I am staggered that anyone could find pleasure in a similar experience. Perhaps if they had my memories of the sight of livid weals across small behinds they would be less amused by such 'erotic' acts.

Richard Billington
Gomshall, Surrey

SIR — I wonder if *Fifty Shades of Grey* would have been so popular with a different title. I have often felt that *The Ancient Mariner*'s huge success was down to the title. *The Old Seaman* may not have had the same effect.

Alan M. Varley
Crowborough, East Sussex

SIR — I grew up in the more romantic and innocent times of the 1950s and 1960s, when young girls had visions of the happy ever after.

I can vividly remember sitting in the staff room of the library where I worked and giggling as the senior assistant read us the saucy bits of *Lady Chatterley's Lover* in our lunch hour. We were quite disappointed at the old-fashioned writing and wondered what all the fuss was about, having had to wait for the Library Committee to pass the book as fit for the public to read.

This was held up for weeks while, it seemed to us, it was read by the council and all their friends. Some returned copies had to go straight for re-binding, so the public were kept waiting even longer.

I do hope that the mainly female readers of

these rather boring 'Shades' books enjoy the much better film. Those who want true erotic fiction and film should stick to the French genre – they seem to know how to do it well, according to the press reviews.

Ann Thompson
Paignton, Devon

SIR – Please could the media write about something other than the shades of grey? Grey does not even feature in the colours of the rainbow. Could we not read about fifty shades of red or yellow or green or blue?

Nothing to do with old age, of course.

Jo Hollis (aged 78)
Middleton, Staffordshire

SIR – At 78 I have absolutely no interest in the film *Fifty Shades of Grey*, but I do want to see *The Lego Movie*, *Paddington* and *Shaun the Sheep: The Movie*.

Does this indicate that I am in my second childhood?

Roy Bailey
Great Shefford, Berkshire

SIR – Sadomasochism is now a regular feature of Prime Minister's Question Time. Ed Miliband begs David Cameron to flog him. David Cameron administers the floggings with relish. Their backbenchers cheer them on. Painful to watch!

Frank Tomlin
Billericay, Essex

THOUGHT FOR THE DAY

SIR – I'm a big fan of the *Today* programme, which I listen to in the car and in the kitchen. I've long wanted to ask: do the distinguished presenters eat their breakfast at the microphone? Of the fabulous five, I'm thinking in particular of James Naughtie. He sometimes has a liquescent, pulpy enunciation that makes me think of a runny fried egg roll. It certainly puts me in the mood for one.

I'd hate to face the team's newest recruit, Mishal Husain, in open court. She is fluent, and can be ferocious. I imagine her a peppermint tea and wholemeal toast person.

I can't say I've ever heard the quintet's doyen, John Humphrys, eat on air, although given his longevity, one might guess he eats muesli with low-fat milk for breakfast – and, of course, politicians.

Martin Ketterer
Glasgow

SIR – With James Naughtie's departure from
the *Today* programme, do you think there will
be a revival of the tried and tested format of the
respondents being given longer to answer the
question than it takes to ask it?

Philip Cole
West Horsley, Surrey

WESTMINSTER'S VILLAGE IDIOTS

POLITICS AT THE SHARP END

SIR – If Alan Johnson, by recommending Thackeray's masterpiece, *Vanity Fair*, can persuade readers to visit the world of avarice, coarseness, duplicity, naked ambition, poverty and riches, all set against the backdrop of the Battle of Waterloo in 1815, he has done a public service.

As for Becky Sharp, it's a good job she is not on the political scene today because she would make mincemeat of the current crop of political pygmies and embroil the nation in scandals that would make the Profumo affair seem like a trivial and titillating escapade.

So enamoured was I with Thackeray's classic that I impetuously purchased a first edition of the novel, and under the malign influence of Becky Sharp was economical with the truth about the cost when subject to questioning by my wife.

If this letter is published I will maintain my dark secret by removing the Letters page before my wife reads the paper and making loud imprecations about the incompetence of the local newsagent, just as the Marquis of Steyne woodcut on page 336 was suppressed in later impressions of the first edition.

Peter Henrick
Birmingham

DARTS OUT FOR BLAIR

SIR — If I were to organise a 'friendly' darts match with a pub in the next village — an event that may require a police presence to avoid bloodshed — the police authority would charge for their services, as they do for a football match or a music festival or other commercial event. Therefore it must be reasonable that Tony Blair should be required to pay for his policing.

In the country we have an old saying: 'If you fly with the rooks, you should expect to get shot at.'

Ian Lewis
Alciston, East Sussex

SIR — The phrase 'the taxpayer' in today's lead story misleadingly suggests that I alone have been funding Tony Blair's globe-trotting activities.

Andrew Blake
Shalbourne, Wiltshire

SIR — Were Mr Blair to be indicted for war crimes the cost of his protection would be significantly reduced.

Judith Barnes
St Ives, Cambridgeshire

SIR – Contrary to your report, it is wholly proper for Tony Blair's company to seek 'assistance from British officials in order to further his private business interests'. I write as someone who spent some time in the 1970s and 1980s encouraging the Foreign Office, who historically thought it rather beneath them, to realise that, in the post 'gunboat' era, it was an important part of their diplomacy.

They are now rather good at it and should be congratulated, not criticised. The attitude of the ambassador who stigmatises this as 'sniffing for work' is half a century out of date.

Mike Thomas
Iver, Buckinghamshire

SIR – Tony Blair is not the first prime minister to exploit the international celebrity brought about by his time in public office. David Lloyd George started the trend when in 1923 he controversially sold his First World War memoirs for a sum today equivalent to £5 million; Winston Churchill continued the trend when in 1946 he sold his Second World War memoirs for a sum equivalent to almost £25 million.

In both cases the lead buyer was one William Berry, later Lord Camrose, as I detail in a forthcoming book *No More Champagne – Churchill and his Money*.

Need I add that from 1927 onwards Lord Camrose was also proprietor and editor-in-chief of *The Daily Telegraph*?

David Lough
Penshurst, Kent

SIR – Am I the only one to have noticed that the answer to Wednesday's polyword puzzle – 'warmonger' – was published on the same day as Tony Blair's resignation as Middle East Peace Envoy?

Roland Matthews
Broadclyst, Devon

SIR – Tony Blair went to the Middle East to do good – and it appears he did very well.

Malcolm Clark
Welwyn, Hertfordshire

SIR – I wouldn't feel so bad over Tony Blair's wealth if he had left the country in a similar state to his own financial wellbeing.

R.D.
Southampton

BUDGET TAKEAWAYS

SIR – Once again, tax cuts in the Budget are being described as a 'give away'. Since it is not their money in the first place, surely the correct description is 'take less'?

John G. Prescott
Coulsdon, Surrey

SIR – What is going on in the Chancellor's mind when he gives the impression of being generous by knocking a penny off a pint?

If I were to survive 50 pints a week – which is unlikely – it wouldn't even buy me a first-class stamp to write him the letter of congratulations on his upcoming part as Scrooge in next Christmas's Commons Panto, should he lose the election.

N.M.
Isle of Arran

SIR – I notice that George Osborne's latest hairstyle is very similar to Rowan Atkinson's. Is it a ploy to bring levity to the proceedings? If so, good on him.

B.S. Scovell
Bromley, Kent

SIR – With inflation forecasted to fall into deflation would this be a good time for the Bank of England to get rid of 1p and 2p coins from circulation? Soon the value of them will be worth more as scrap.

Jonathan Batt
Castle Cary, Somerset

SIR – I note that Starbucks has disclosed that it has made its first profit after trading for 16 years in the UK. Is it safe to assume that its coffee is at last drinkable?

David Miller
Maidenhead, Kent

BONUSES FOR SMUG TAXPAYERS

SIR – With some 10,000 pages of tax legislation it is scarcely surprising that some payers miss HMRC's deadline and get fined.

Surely HMRC are missing a trick. Why do they not offer a £100 bonus for those returns filed before July 31, and £50 before October 31? The results would be miraculous.

Having just filed my own return for the first time before the scramble at the end of January, I am feeling quite smug and would welcome an incentive.

Warwick Banks
Allington, Lincolnshire

SIR – The UK GDP figures have recently taken to including revenue from prostitution and drug dealing. In the event that I find myself visiting a prostitute, or buying crack cocaine from a dealer round the corner, should I demand a receipt or otherwise insist on paying by cheque, in order to avoid encouraging tax evasion?

Quentin Skinner
Warminster, Wiltshire

GENUINE BALLS

SIR – When I pay someone £10 cash to cut my hedge, Ed Balls wants me to obtain a receipt showing the gardener's name and address. As I will have paid out of taxed income what, pray, am I meant to do with the receipt? And remind me, what is the amount under which MPs do not have to provide receipts for their expenses claims?

The only genuine thing about Ed Balls is his name.

Robert Chatterton
Caythorpe, Lincolnshire

SIR – I would be most grateful if Mr Balls could give me the name of a gardener who cuts hedges for £10. I would gladly pay his travel costs to Dover. My last bill for hedge-cutting was in excess of £200 – and I did obtain a receipt.

Philip Barry
Lydden, Kent

SIR – Can Mr Balls confirm that he issued a receipt when he and his then boss Gordon Brown sold most of the country's gold reserves at rock bottom prices, against the best economic advice?

John Sorrell
Paris, France

SIR – Here in the rugged colony we consider ourselves pretty unshockable, but we were astonished that Mr Balls would blatantly admit to getting receipts for hand jobs. Your MPs' expenses are clearly well out of control again.

Tim Parker
Sydney, Australia

HOUSE OF CRACKPOTS

SIR – Sir Peter Tapsell has warned that 'If people in this house are not allowed a second job, membership of it will soon be largely confined to the inheritors of substantial fortunes, or to rich spouses or to obsessive crackpots, or to those who are unemployable anywhere else.'

Is it not already?

Gary Williamson
Kingston, Surrey

SIR – Rather than calling for MPs to be banned from having a second job might it be more to the benefit of the country, and to Parliament, not to say more of a vote winner, if Ed Miliband called for all MPs to have held a first job?

Andrew Wildblood
London SW6

SIR – Perhaps MPs should be placed on zero-hour contracts, thus allowing them time for other pursuits.

Nicola Turton
Lychpit, Hampshire

SIR – If, after over 30 years of collecting the salaries of MPs and ministers, Sir Malcolm Rifkind and Jack Straw do not have enough money to live on, they are not competent to be trusted with the affairs of the nation. If they do, they are too greedy to be permitted to retain their seats.

Revd Richard Haggis
Oxford

SIR – The thing that worries me about people like Rifkind and Straw is that they do not realise just how much £8,000 is for just half a day's work. I accept that Rifkind is a Conservative but Straw should know better.

J. Wright
Kirkella, East Yorkshire

SIR – How does one refer oneself to the Parliamentary Standards Committee? I ask because apparently it's what you should do if you've done nothing wrong.

A.M. Barwani
London N11

SIR – Surely the latest scandal tells us that too many Members of Parliament serve for far too long in their seats. PMQs indicates that some are there for entertainment value only. I am often shocked by the sight of a faded figure, whom I thought had died years ago, still resting on the benches.

MPs should be required to relinquish their seats after 10 years or so. They could then go out into the world and use their undoubted talents to make some serious money, after which they would be allowed back, no longer needing to make something on the side.

Brian Farmer
Chelmsford, Essex

BLUNT WORDS

SIR – Good for James Blunt and his response to Chris Bryant. Mr Bryant should realise that however creativity is arrived at, it's good for our society. James Blunt is not just a lucky posh boy, any more

than was van Gogh, Isaac Newton or Shakespeare.
I'm not a fan of his music, but I do admire him as
a person. Chris Bryant, on the other hand, is a . . .
politician.

Brenden Dyke
Gravesend, Kent

SIR — 'Gimp' is a word that was new to me, so I read
James Blunt's letter to learn more.
It is only a letter — not a Byron poem or a Sheridan
play or a Churchill speech or a Curtis script — but
it was good to see that his posh and privileged
boarding school can still deliver The Three Rs.

Dr John Simpson
Balrath, County Meath

BLOOD, SWEAT, TOIL AND CIGARS

SIR — I have been so moved this week by the
anniversary of Winston Churchill's death, a
reminder of his many achievements and how
marvellous he made England feel. It would be an
excellent way of saying thank you to allow one day
when you can smoke a cigar in public. I have never
smoked but I would give this one a whirl.

Rosemary Almond
Hoddesdon, Hertfordshire

SIR – When nursing Sir Winston in the Middlesex Hospital following his leg fracture, I popped a thermometer in his mouth. One minute later he removed the thermometer and handed it back to me.

I said, 'Thank you, Sir Winston.'

His reply, in a deep baritone voice, looking me straight in the eye: 'I am thanking you for thanking me.'

Very Churchillian?

Ann Harvard Davis
Ringmer, East Sussex

SIR – Fifty years after the burial of our greatest ever wartime leader the nation grinds to a halt at the lightest flurry of snow. I despair; what has become of the bulldog spirit?

Dr Bertie Dockerill
Shildon, County Durham

SIR – Before rushing to rename Heathrow Airport after Sir Winston Churchill, as your correspondent suggests, perhaps we should heed the wisdom of that most authoritative arbiter of taste Margo, Lady Metroland.

She said of Paris streets named after French leaders words to the effect: '[Britain] should never follow the example of using our great men for the mere convenience of postmen.'

The emotional spasm that turned the poetic 'Idlewild' airport into the topical 'Kennedy' became the banal 'JFK' almost immediately. If Heathrow was re-named Churchill, how long before it became WSC?

To have the name Churchill reduced to a convenient shorthand for a sprawling tourist and retail hub would be bad enough. To tamper with British history and culture would be worse.

Ivan Rendall
Kings Green, Worcestershire

WELCOME TO LONDON CALAIS

SIR – Just how far to the south-east is the country's principal airport expected to be? Why not go the whole hog and put it in the wastelands of northern France? It's a lot easier for 40 million of us in the UK to fly to the world via Paris or Schiphol than to meander across Europe's most expensive rail system to something on the distant, most inaccessible side of London.

Chris Wood
York

SIR – As the HS2 journey time from London to Manchester is claimed to be about the same as the Piccadilly Line from King's Cross to Heathrow, London's next runway should be built in Manchester.

Robert Perks
Lytham St Annes, Lancashire

SIR – My grandmother, who was born in 1887, always referred to Heathrow as 'the London Airplane Station'.

Angela Clifford
Epsom, Surrey

SIR – Heathrow or Gatwick? If we were in China both would be constructed and operational by Christmas, with back-ups at Stansted and Luton by Easter. It's time we woke up.

J. David
Welwyn Garden City, Hertfordshire

SIR – Heathrow gets my vote because it offers four hours free internet while Gatwick offers only a miserly 90 minutes.

Michael J. Fay
Tortola, British Virgin Islands

SIR – One solution would be to use Heathrow only for business travellers. All holiday makers would have to use the other airports in the provinces for their travel arrangements.

Gerald Milne
Windsor, Berkshire

SIR – I normally avoid Heathrow like the plague for long-haul flights but in the past 12 months I have used it twice. On each occasion we were transferred by bus to and from the terminal. Maybe they should just add a third lane to the bus route?

Brian J. Singleton
Baslow, Derbyshire

NEW DIRECTION FOR CAMERON

SIR – The announcements that David Cameron will not serve a third term as Prime Minister and Zayn Malik is leaving One Direction are almost too much to bear in only a few days. Could it be that the third piece of tragic news is that Ed Miliband is resigning?

Brian Lait
Maroni, Cyprus

SIR – Where were you when you heard that Zayn was leaving One Direction?

Michael Carton
Ickenham, Middlesex

SIR – I wish to volunteer as a replacement. I can't sing and, when I dance, I can only go in one direction. I should be ideal.

Robin Nonhebel
Swanage, Dorset

SIR – I am not a fan, but would it not be sensible for the group, having lost a quarter of their membership, to be renamed No Direction?

Charles Dobson
Burton-in-Kendal, Cumbria

THE LONG, BUMPY ROAD TO MAY 7

SIR – Clearly an election approaches. Potholes are being filled in.

Alan Banton
Chorleywood, Hertfordshire

SIR – My International Day of Happiness started with my husband ranting at the political interview on the *Today* programme, and then storming out of the bedroom after I asked him to calm down. Will our 43-year marriage survive this election?

Gillian S.S. Lambert
Tadworth, Surrey

SIR – Why is it that, when a general election is called, I campaign enthusiastically for weeks, but after each campaign my wife is returned to power without so much as a recount?

Peter Wyton
Longlevens, Gloucestershire

SIR – How many lies can the human brain absorb within five weeks without exploding? I fear mine is reaching the limit.

Peter le Feuvre
Funtington, West Sussex

SIR – David Cameron has said he wants dementia cured by 2025. Is he campaigning for Prime Minister or a Sainthood?

Kirsty Blunt
Sedgeford, Norfolk

SIR – Have I got this right? David Cameron promises council tenants the right to buy their rented property at below market value provided he gets enough votes. Meanwhile, a UKIP candidate hands round a plate of sausage rolls – and the police investigate the UKIP candidate for potentially bribing voters.

H. Alexander
Hambledon, Surrey

SIR – Eight billion pounds to improve the NHS? What most patients want is a bed pan on demand.

Tobias Hitman
London W5

SIR – I feel as if I have visited two car showrooms where both sets of sales staff have told me that the car they plan to market meets all my personal needs, but neither are able to set out exactly how much the vehicle will cost or what specification will actually be delivered.

Roger Gentry
Sutton-at-Hone, Kent

SIR – I have recently had a severe attack of labyrinthitis. When I get up out of a chair I always lurch to the left. Is this an omen for the election result? Does anyone know how to change the direction of lurch to the right, my favoured direction?

J. Geoffrey Innes
Niton, Isle of Wight

SIR – Can anyone predict the result? So far as I can see, it's between the Conservative Party and the BBC.

Paul Craddock
Stalbridge, Dorset

SIR – One might as well scrap the monarchy and install Jeremy Paxman as president on May 7.

John Sabin
Pulborough, West Sussex

SIR – Today's edition of *The Daily Telegraph* has eight pages of Tory propaganda, an obvious sign of panic in the ranks. Roll on next week when you can fill the pages with advertisements again.

G.P.-H.
Preston, Lancashire

SIR – Who cares who wins the general election? Is there really a single MP who says or does anything differently to any of the others? The whole thing should be ignored. That way we really will get a change.

Stefan Badham
Paulsgrove, Hampshire

STUMPED ON THE STUMP

SIR – No parliamentary candidate has passed my front-gate initiative test. The electric-powered five-bar gate bears a keypad, on which is written 'Press to open'.

I have seen canvassers fail to deliver their leaflets and callers defeated by this simple instruction.

Manifestos are left in the woodwork but no one has reached my door.

All of this proves to me that our politicians don't press the right buttons.

David Leech
Balcombe, West Sussex

SIR – My father stood as a Conservative Parliamentary Candidate in Bilston in the 1950 general election.

One of his favourite stories involved knocking on a door after a day of campaigning to be greeted by an elderly lady who promised that she would definitely vote for him.

When asked why she replied: 'You have a Bulldog and I love Bulldogs.'

Jonathan E. Godrich
Clee St Margaret, Shropshire

SIR – Our dog Ben has savaged all electioneering material pushed through our letterbox, with the exception of any communication from the Conservative Party. My son even tried reposting the same flyer, but still no mauling from Ben. Are we to conclude that our dog swings to the right?

Sally Hudson
Tilehurst, Berkshire

SIR – One of the benefits of all this election drivel coming through the letterbox is that it's great for fire lighting.

Janet Wilson
Weaverham, Cheshire

I SLEPT WITH CAMERON'S MOTHER

SIR – I shall be awfully disappointed if David Cameron loses the election as it will deprive me of my only political conversation stopper when arguments about our Prime Minister get heated at dinner parties.

'Of course,' I say, casually, 'I slept with his mother.'

The stunned silence which follows is always most gratifying, although I then have to explain that his mother, nee Mary Mount, was a fellow pupil at my boarding school.

Heather Spink
Dallington, East Sussex

SIR – Speaking in the kitchen about her husband, Samantha Cameron said that she hopes that 'Me and the family – me and the children – help him to keep things in perspective.'

Me hope so too; and me wonder also if her Marlborough College education was all it should have been.

Martin Burgess
Beckenham, Kent

SIR — Your lead story today has a photograph of Mr Cameron with shirtsleeves rolled up, preaching to the workers. However, the fact he has no breast pocket shows that he is truly a toff.

David Hall
Banstead, Surrey

SIR — My opinion of David Cameron fell from 9.5 to 0 on a 10-point scale after I read about him 'sitting on a rickety plastic chair with a hot dog topped with lashings of ketchup'.

Every connoisseur of hot dogs knows that they cry out to be topped with mustard (Gulden's, if available).

William Harrell
Stone Cross, East Sussex

TORY PRIMARIES

SIR – Has anyone else noticed that the politicians seem to be doing all their canvassing in primary schools? Is it because their audiences can't answer back? They certainly can't vote.

Ann Collings
Surbiton, Surrey

SIR – One feels totally disconnected these days from politicians; you don't get much of a chance to shout at them.

During the 1964 election I was one of two teenage hecklers outside the Kirkdale pub in Sydenham as Sir Alec Douglas-Home addressed a large crowd about unemployment.

Similarly, in Leicester in 1974 I remember going to a public meeting where hundreds of people were crowded into an auditorium to listen to Harold Wilson speak. He walked to the stage within touching distance of those at the end of the rows of seats. Anyone and everyone could be there. How he dealt with hecklers was a treat.

David Silver
Wisbech, Cambridgeshire

SIR – The Conservatives are living in cloud-cuckoo-land if they believe Boris Johnson will make a good party leader and Prime Minister.

I have a lot of time for Boris, but his cultivated bumbledom image, his penchant for scooting around a capital on two wheels and his dubious personal life make him more suited to the Presidency of France.

Keith Haines
Belfast

SIR – Reading John Major's thoughts in the *Telegraph* make me think that he was probably the best Prime Minister we never knew we had.

Graham Bond
Matching Green, Essex

SIR – What on earth will David Cameron and George Osborne do with their Bob the Builder outfits after the election? Will we see two hi-vis jackets and yellow hard hats for sale on eBay?

Philip Moger
East Preston, West Sussex

WHEELS COMING OFF LABOUR'S PINK BUS

SIR – Has anyone noticed the similarity between Harriet Harman's pink bus and the adverts for Ann

Summers parties? Not only is the colour the same but they are both for women only.

If I was allowed in, I know which one I would choose.

Stephen Barklem
Woking, Surrey

SIR – For one horrible moment I thought that, to appeal to women voters, Harriet Harman had unveiled her pink bust.

Geoff Milburn
Glossop, Derbyshire

SIR – Surely the bus should have been painted fifty shades of grey?

Bob Stebbings
Chorleywood, Hertfordshire

SIR –

The workers' flag was deepest red
To symbolise their martyrs dead.
Now Labour's bus is painted pink,
Enough to drive poor Marx to drink.

Chris Chick
Holbrook, Suffolk

SIR – The baby boomer in me is reminded of a brand of pink bicycle popular in the 1950s. To bolster Labour's environmental and health credentials, might we soon see politicians cycling around on replica 'Pink Witch' bikes?

Remember where you heard it first — may one get a Peerage for such ideas?

Revd Canon Alan Hughes
Wark, Northumberland

SIR — The wheels must be well and truly coming off Labour's election campaign if Ed Miliband is resorting to employing John Prescott as his spokesman on climate change. How typical of Labour that they appoint a windbag full of hot air to the climate change portfolio.

Adrian Stockwell
Farnham, Surrey

DEBATING MILIBAND'S FLAWS

SIR — It is extremely worrying to see that someone aspiring to be the Prime Minister of the United Kingdom has such a poor command of our language.

In last night's television debate Ed Miliband asked David Cameron to 'Debate me, debate me'. I fail to see why Mr Cameron would wish to enter a debate on the subject of Mr Miliband.

Philippa Madgwick
Glastonbury, Somerset

SIR – If Stephanie Flanders found a few weeks with Ed Miliband to be 'very costly', how expensive will a five-year relationship be?

Victor Montefiore
London NW7

SIR – Am I unusual in repeatedly misreading #milifandom as 'milf and dom'? Makes you wonder who will have the whip hand.

Allan Reese
Forston, Dorset

SIR – On the radio Ed Miliband sounds just like one of the flowerpot men Bill or Ben.

Robert Stevenson
Cheltenham, Gloucestershire

SIR – My anagram of Edward Samuel Miliband is 'I am weird and "um" Ed Balls'.

B.J.
London SE22

SIR – As the two Eds cannot remember what to say, what their policies are, and who funds them, they shouldn't be too surprised if we do not remember to vote for them.

Brian Christley
Abergele, Conwy

SIR – Although I don't have a lot of time for Labour politicians I do sympathise with the difficulty some of them are having in remembering names. My late wife used to tell friends that even in introducing her, I sometimes hesitated. She was waiting for the time when she was introduced as 'Umm Errh'.

Even associating names with everyday things can have unfortunate outcomes. Someone named Elizabeth can perhaps be remembered by visualising her with a crown on her head, but introduce her as Queenie and you are lost.

Bill Scott
Mawnan Smith, Cornwall

SIR – Ed Miliband debating with Russell Brand! George Osborne playing with sheep! Surely we have finally plumbed the depths in these pathetic daily p***ing contests that pass for electioneering. Whatever happened to statesmen? Heaven help us.

Den Beves
Pennant, Powys

SIR – At long last Ed Miliband has found his political brother.

Adrian Thompson
Monk Bretton, South Yorkshire

SIR – So now we know why Mr Miliband is so keen to cut energy bills – he has to power two kitchens. Silly me – I thought he was going to do it for our benefit.

Philip Coulson
Dunkirk, Kent

SIR – Ed Miliband's second kitchen must be the one he uses to practise eating bacon sandwiches.

John Tilsiter
Radlett, Hertfordshire

SIR – What additional kitchen used merely for the 'preparation of tea and quick snacks' requires a double oven?

Jean Knipe
London SE11

SIR – Kitchens are so last month. I would like to suggest bathrooms next. The Greens would no doubt like us all to squat on the compost heap, Labour probably still prefers the purpose-built brick hut in the garden, while no doubt the Conservatives and the Liberals favour combining the loo and the bathroom within the house.

Taken all round I think I will support the coalition view. No photos necessary in this instance.

Judith A. Scott
St. Ives, Cambridgeshire

DOUBLE, DOUBLE, TOIL AND TROUBLE

SIR — Watching the embracing huddle of Nicola Sturgeon, Natalie Bennett and Leanne Wood at the end of the television debate, I thought it bore a striking resemblance to Act I, Scene I of the Scottish play.

Richard Craven
Pickering, North Yorkshire

SIR — If it were not a proven fact that Natalie Bennett, Leader of the Green Party, actually exists, I would have suspected her of being a character dreamt up by Peter Simple.

Nigel Milliner
Tregony, Cornwall

SIR — Your photograph of Mr Miliband's shoes in the leaders' debate reveal a reason good enough in itself not to vote for him. We all know not to trust a man in pointy shoes, but those square-fronted ones are just as appalling.

Rory Buchanan
Charney Bassett, Oxfordshire

SIR – Many years ago, when I was a young shoe salesman, I was told by wise and experienced hands that you do not bring out more than three shoes at a time for a customer. If they want to see more, you bring one or two, but you also remove one or two. If there is a large selection to choose from, the customer usually ends up confused and undecided, with the end result being no sale.

As I watched the televised political debate between salespeople of the seven political parties, all I could see on the screen were the words 'No Sale'.

J. Martin
West Bergholt, Essex

SIR – I forgot to tune in to the election debate and instead watched *MasterChef* and a documentary called *The Truth About Fat*. There were no recipes for disaster and at least I got to learn the truth about something.

Phil Warner
Alvechurch, Warwickshire

SIR – If Tony Blair had participated in a televised political debate he would have won it hands down. What does that tell us about the process?

Mick Ferrie
Mawnan Smith, Cornwall

SIR – Might I suggest that instead of televising pre-election debates, the BBC shows a repeat of *Yes, Prime Minister*. This is far more likely to enable all of us to make an informed decision about which way to vote on May 7.

Bruce Chalmers
Goring by Sea, West Sussex

SIR – Could Nicola Sturgeon be persuaded to take a drop in salary and become Prime Minister of Great Britain?

Rob Reynolds
Staplefield, West Sussex

NICOLA STURGEON VS THE ENGLISH

SIR – It seems Nicola Sturgeon has a poor grasp of English. She keeps referring to 'progressive' policies, when she means 'profligate' policies.

B.W. Jervis
Sheffield

SIR – Why is it that the Scottish accent no longer reassures?

Tim Deane
Tisbury, Wiltshire

SIR – For many years my husband has blamed our much-loved, long-dead cat Smokey for all that has gone wrong in the world. Now he is blaming Nicola Sturgeon. I think perhaps he might be right.

Felicity M. Smith
Cheadle Hulme, Cheshire

SIR – It seems we might end up having the country held to ransom by a combination of Russell Brand and Nicola Sturgeon, neither of whom is even standing for Parliament. Perhaps the unelected EU Commissioners are not so bad after all?

Ian Walter
Ley Hill, Buckinghamshire

SIR – Has anyone noticed the resemblance between Alex Salmond and Silvio Berlusconi? Should the Scots be worried? Or indeed the Italians?

Bob Stebbings
Chorleywood, Hertfordshire

SIR – Nicola Sturgeon increasingly resembles a doll removed from its plastic-fronted box and endlessly repeating the string-pull statement: 'Tory Welfare Cuts'.

As with the toy, if those three words were removed from her vocabulary, she would be struck dumb.

Malcolm Parkin
Kinnesswood, Kinross-shire

SIR – For heaven's sake, where is Cameron's fighting character? He acts like a right wimp in a baby bath with Nanny washing under his arms. Sturgeon has thrown down the gauntlet. Pick it up, Cameron, and be a man.

She is blowing and blustering. Take the initiative, if you are capable. Bin the Barnett formula forthwith, ban SNP votes in Parliament for English affairs and ensure that all taxes come to the central pot.

Call her bluff. Good lord, she is not even an MP, so kick her into the side-lines where she belongs. It is exactly what she is doing to you, you clot.

Lt Col Dale Hemming-Tayler (retd)
Edith Weston, Rutland

SIR – Against all the odds I wish to say a word for Nicola Sturgeon. Where all other means have failed she, with Alex Salmond's help, has succeeded in curing my life-long addiction to Scotch whisky. Considering my hitherto formidable reputation in that field I regard this as no mean achievement.

Donald Morrison
Woodbridge, Suffolk

SIR – I read that the Queen technically owns all sturgeons, whales and dolphins. I am sure that she is delighted to own the latter two, but may wish to speak firmly to one of the first.

Gay Fearn
Haywards Heath, West Sussex

SIR – Nicola Sturgeon: now I know how many people felt about Margaret Thatcher.

Richard Statham
Langport, Somerset

SIR – In financial terms the SNP bid to 'control' England would be known as a reverse takeover. These are usually of great benefit as a funding vehicle to the small company but of doubtful benefit to the large undertaking they are trying to control.

To continue the analogy, I recommend the English shareholders reject this offer.

Moira Brodie FCA
Bourton, Oxfordshire

SIR – I climbed Snowdon last year with my wife, daughter and son-in-law. At the summit we enjoyed a hot chocolate at the cafe to fight off the chill outdoors.

We climbed Scafell Pike over the bank holiday weekend but were sorely disappointed not to find the same facility there. 1-0 to the Welsh.

Ben Nevis is planned for September, so I have duly written to Ms Sturgeon asking if Scotland is up to speed with the Welsh and ahead of the English. I am awaiting her reply.

She promised just about everything else in the Scottish referendum so this surely would be child's play. She has three months to get it implemented.

John Rowlands
Harpenden, Hertfordshire

SIR – If Ed and Nicola end up in bed together, can you imagine what ghastly offspring will emerge from that reluctant coupling?

All we can hope for is a military coup, restoring the divine right of Charles III to rule unhindered by the Commons.

Mike Lightfoot
Hutton Bonville, North Yorkshire

HAPPY POLLING DAY

SIR – I am surprised that in this commercial world in which we live, we are not able to send 'Happy Polling Day' cards to our friends and local politicians.

Russ King
London N11

SIR – Having read my poll card which stated that I was not required to take it with me to vote, I duly presented myself at the polling station and gave my name to the official at the desk. I confirmed that I lived at a certain address, and was given the ballot paper.

I asked the officials how they knew that I was who I said I was. No one had an answer, and so I left, with three bemused keepers of our democracy sitting open-mouthed.

How trusting we British are.

Stanford Allen
London NW11

SIR – Had you acted on my letter of April 23 and placed £30,000 on a Tory win you might be collecting a £240,000 cheque from Ladbrokes.

Duncan Rayner
Sunningdale, Berkshire

SIR – Up to and including polling day, my inbox was filled with increasingly plaintive pleas from the likes of David Cameron, Boris Johnson and William Hague imploring me to vote Conservative. Since the election, not a whisper. Where is the expression of gratitude? Where is the display of good manners?

Dr J.P.G. Bolton
Taunton, Somerset

SIR – As our new daughter arrived on May 6,
I assume that my vote today carried extra weight
owing to the fact that we can regard ourselves
as a 'hard-working family'. I distinctly recall
being half of a feckless couple last week.

Anthony Gordon
London E14

SIR – It seems David Cameron was right in his
verbal slip when he suggested it was to be a 'career
changing election'. Mr Clegg and Mr Miliband will
now need to join the 'hard-working families' and
find out what those words really mean.

Peter Ferguson Western
Poole, Dorset

SIR – Your photo of Mhairi Black, the new
20-year-old SNP MP, with her plate of chips,
should be a salutary reminder to those in the
Labour Party responsible for the selection of
Parliamentary candidates how important it is to
choose someone with a background of 'real-life'
experience, wise in the ways of tweeting.

Incidentally, judging by the percentage swings
north of the border, the plate of chips would
probably have beaten Douglas Alexander.

Dave Bacon
Vale, Guernsey

SIR – Most observers have missed the simple reason Labour lost the election. People do not die in the mines, mills and foundries every day like they did a century ago.

Like a radioactive isotope the Labour Party has a half-life of approximately five years and will be the size of the Lib Dems after the next election, the Greens the election after that and then disappear.

Mark Harland
Scarborough, North Yorkshire

SIR – Is it likely that Ed Miliband will now be best remembered for his all-too-prescient words, 'No, no, it ain't gonna happen'?

Reg Gutteridge
Nottingham

SIR – Perhaps Mr Miliband should consider recycling his Moses tablet into a new worktop for one of his kitchens. He would then be able to eat his words, off his own words; these may be more tasteful to him than haggis.

Andrew McAllister
Shrewsbury

SIR – Perhaps he should enter his monolith manifesto for the Turner Prize?

B. Marshall
Fundenhall, Norfolk

SIR – Having read PPE at Oxford and now having a bit of spare time, Mr Miliband should re-enrol and concentrate on the 'E' bit again. I'm not sure he really got it the first time.

Christopher Leach
Thorpe Bay, Essex

SIR – I gather that due to removal of the spectre of the Labour mansion tax, Savills are predicting a whopping 23 per cent increase in the value of London properties currently worth over £1.5 million. Ed Miliband must be quietly pleased.

Donald Keir
Aberdeen

SIR – The people I feel sorry for are Ed Balls and Yvette Cooper. How are they going to manage on only one set of parliamentary expenses?

A.J. Watson
Harraton, County Durham

SIR – When we raise our glasses in celebration we no longer say 'Cheers' or 'Prost' or 'Bottoms up'. We just say 'Balls'.

A.R.
Worcester

SIR – I belong to a women's craft group which has met for a number of years in the upstairs offices of the local Liberal Democrats. We came downstairs after our meeting last night to find that a member of the electorate had silently voiced his opinion of the party by urinating through the letter box.

> **G.R.**
> Merseyside

SIR – Two men resigned as party leader last Friday. I have a small observation on the character of these two men. On the Monday, one goes on holiday to Ibiza leaving his two small children behind; the other I witnessed helping his small son onto his bicycle and going for a ride with him after school.

I didn't vote for either of them, incidentally.

> **J.G.**
> London SW15

SIR – I have been most impressed with the post-election speeches of defeated candidates and resigning leaders. They were humbly delivered, heartfelt and considered. If only they had delivered their election addresses in the same way the people may have been more receptive.

> **Malcolm Allen**
> Berkhamsted, Hertfordshire

SIR – The resignation speeches of Clegg, Miliband and Farage call to mind Wolsey's Farewell. Suitably adapted, each could have lamented:

I have ventured,
Like little wanton boys that swim on bladders,
This many summers in a sea of glory.
Vain pomp and glory of this world I hate ye:
Oh how wretched
Is that poor man that hangs on voters' favours!
And when he falls he falls like Lucifer,
Never to hope again.

John Bromley-Davenport
Malpas, Cheshire

SIR – Just wondering if the fallout from the general election could solve the BBC's question of the new presenters for *Top Gear*: Miliband, Clegg and Farage.

Debbie King
Tissington, Derbyshire

SIR – Am I alone in detecting a sense of the inevitable in the rejection of Mr Farage's resignation by the board of UKIP? Can he not be more persistent?

W.J. Farren
Sevenoaks, Kent

SIR – Patrick O'Flynn, UKIP MEP and election campaign chief, has described Nigel Farage as 'thin-skinned'. Oh, do pull the other one. I doubt it would be possible to mark Nigel with a pickaxe. And no wonder he has hissy fits, surrounded as he is by such numpties.

He obviously needs a course in stress management at the Gordon Brown School of Telephone Throwing.

Patrick Tracey
Carlisle

OFFAL OPINION POLLS

SIR – When divining the future the ancient Babylonians used sheep's livers; the Romans, birds; the Renaissance Europeans, astrology; and we, expensively crunched statistics. Yet predictively speaking, they are all about equal.

Could I suggest, therefore, that before the next election, we get some white-bearded elderly gentlemen to make incantations over some butchers' offal. It would be much cheaper than opinion polls. And probably more accurate.

Dr Allan Chapman
Oxford, Oxfordshire

SIR – I'm pleased to note that I am not the only person in the country who tells pollsters the opposite of what I intend to do.

Alexander Johnston
Syston, Leicestershire

SIR – I am sorry; I hate the BBC as much as anyone, but this 'shy Tory' business will not do. It is clearly not correct. The idea that there is a million-strong army of shrinking violets too morally paralysed to tell a nice young lady with a clipboard that they might vote Conservative, who then, inspired by the thrill of the franchise, bound out of the polling booth and tell an exit pollster that they did is nonsense.

Where are they intimidated? When they go to buy their *Daily Mail* in the morning and see their local plumber buying his copy of the *Sun*? Playing cribbage with their mates in the pub? Watching football matches or *The X Factor* on television? At the bowls match?

You are offering a ridiculous image of your own people. No, I am afraid that they all said 'undecided' because they hadn't decided yet. And quite right, too. It is an important decision.

Paul Jones
Radcliffe-on-Trent, Nottinghamshire

BOTTOM-LINE WHIP

SIR – What other employer would advertise a job at a published salary then allow the lucky recipients to vote themselves a pay rise as one of their first duties?

Chris Semple
Rownhams, Hampshire

SIR – In light of the fact that MPs are going to get a 10 per cent pay rise I would be happier if I knew that they weren't slacking in their job.

My last employment was with a computer manufacturer. The IT department made available on the internal website, on a monthly basis, a list of all internet domain names accessed by the staff. It didn't stop people using non-work-related websites, but if you knew that your use was being logged, it might make you think twice about doing so.

Personally, I'd like to see how many times Facebook, eBay, Amazon and the like are accessed from within the Palace of Westminster, let alone Candy Crush Saga.

Steve Webb
Southwell, Nottinghamshire

SIR – As the House of Commons requires repairs, could we not moor our new aircraft carrier (which has no planes) next to the Parliament buildings as an alternative Chamber and perhaps allow it to gently float away?

Greg Dunningham
Swindon, Wiltshire

RIP, CHARLES KENNEDY

SIR – Most modern leaders all seem to have brilliant marriages, clever children, go running four days a week, drink 14 units a week, and eat their five-a-day. Charles Kennedy didn't, and I liked that.

William Rusbridge
Tregony, Cornwall

SIR – With regard to the news that Charles Kennedy was on the cusp of a life peerage, Sir Humphrey Appleby was prophetic some 30 years ago: 'I gather that he was as drunk as Lord. So, after a discreet interval, they will probably make him one.'

Michael Liddell
Chipping Norton, Oxfordshire

CORBYN FOR LABOUR LEADER

SIR – The election of Jeremy Corbyn as Labour leader would be a great thing. It would confirm that Labour, like the men-only Garrick, is a private club in which like-minded members can live happily together in a closed-off ideological community, while remaining a total irrelevance to the rest of us living in the real world.

Victor Launert
Matlock Bath, Derbyshire

SIR – Yvette Cooper refuses to admit that Labour overspent but still sees herself as a suitable candidate for leader of the Labour Party. This, and indeed her choice of spouse, is indicative of her complete lack of judgement.

Juliet Henderson
South Warnborough, Hampshire

SIR – If it should come down to a choice between Yvette Cooper and Andy Burnham to become leader of the Labour Party, will it be decided by who can conjure up the most plaintive of expressions when asked about the NHS or the minimum wage?

David Partington
Higher Walton, Cheshire

SIR – Would it not be quicker to elect Len McCluskey as leader of the Labour Party?

Roger Davies
Boxted, Essex

SIR – Labour MP Andy Burnham has been mocked by some on the Left for his somewhat unctuous form of sign-off in a letter to Prince Charles. Perhaps he should have taken a leaf out of the book of the Duke of Wellington, whose formal sign-off on one occasion stated, 'I remain Sir, your most obedient servant . . .', followed by the words '. . . though you know damned well I am not'.

Ted Shorter
Hildenborough, Kent

SIR – Why do so many modern Labour MPs shorten their forenames? Imagine Clem Atlee, Harry Wilson or Mike Foot.

And who might we look forward to after Andy has left the political stage? Del Boy, perhaps?

Anthony Tuck
Dawlish, Devon

SIR – Surely no self-respecting Labour supporter will wish to have their leader called Tristram?

Stephen Hitch
Ermington, Devon

SIR – Tristram Hunt has stated that all teachers must be qualified. I ask: what qualifications are required to be an MP?

John Christoffersen
Cleethorpes, Lincolnshire

SIR – As does Chuka Umunna, I wore Savile Row
suits when at work. The difference between us is that
mine fitted.

Jeremy Haworth
Aldermaston, Berkshire

FLIPPING A DESERT ISLAND

SIR – Can there be any more appropriate
candidates for sending to an uninhabited desert
island than Mr and Mrs Bercow – assuming, of
course, that they wouldn't be able to claim it as
their second home and refurbish it at the taxpayers'
expense?

Tony Lank
Hurstpierpoint, West Sussex

SIR – I am not too fussed whether *The Daily Telegraph*
fully covered all the issues regarding HSBC
alleged tax misconduct. I am, however, extremely
disappointed you failed to brighten my day by
reporting the recent ski slope misfortunes of Sally
Bercow.

Ken Wilson
Birmingham

SIR – David Cameron has just comfortably won a general election, his political rivals have all resigned and now John Bercow has been publicly humiliated. Is anyone else wondering if the grateful genie Mr Cameron clearly freed from his lamp has only granted him the traditional three wishes or has he thrown in a few extra ones to boot?

Cai Ross
Llandudno Junction, Conwy

CAMERON'S EURO VISION

SIR – In his negotiations with the European Union David Cameron must take some encouragement from the fact that of the 28 competitors' songs in the Eurovision Song Contest finals, 23 were in English.

Paul Strong
Claxby, Lincolnshire

SIR – Might the wording of the EU referendum be expanded to the question of our continued participation in the Eurovision Song Contest?

David Docherty
London W4

SIR – In Saturday's Eurovision Song Contest, Germany and Austria finished joint last with 'nul points' each. Quite right, too – these countries totally lack any musical tradition.

Robin Stieber
London SW6

SIR – 'Blair to speak out in favour of EU membership', you report. What a tremendous boost for the 'No' campaign.

Jim Sanderson
Hapton, Lancashire

SIR – Iain Duncan Smith, the former Conservative leader, says that he has campaigned for a referendum on the European Union for 24 years.

Not exactly a track record of success.

Sandy Pratt
Dormansland, Surrey

FARAGE OF ARABIA

SIR – It has become clear in recent times that British establishment figures have united in a common cause to humiliate and belittle Nigel Farage and UKIP at every opportunity. This reminds me of the way in which T.E. Lawrence was dismissed by the British military establishment in the early 20th century whenever he had the audacity to challenge their plans. Had they listened to Lawrence, we most certainly would not have the festering mess that we have today in what was then called Palestine.

I hope that in 50 years' time our history books do not have the story about how much better Britain would have been had the establishment had the common sense to listen to Nigel Farage and his fellow Ukippers.

Ian Johnson
Chelford, Cheshire

HOME
THOUGHTS ON
ABROAD

ENTENTES CORDIALES

SIR – I am a foreigner who has lived in England for many years. As your article suggests, the combination of a French husband and an English wife usually ends in tears.

I like English women very much, and have spent much of my life with them. They are attractive, they have good figures and they are less calculating than French women. So they are ideal mistresses. But by our standards, they are rotten wives, because they do not know how to keep house and they are always bolting.

However, the other way round, a French wife and an English husband, works very well, because the English husband is looked after in a way he never dreamed of; French women know how to keep their husbands happy.

I have never been to bed with an English man, but all English women tell me they are not very good lovers. Still, with a French wife, they might improve.

> **D.P. M.**
> London SW1

SIR – It seems that there might be life on other planets. Should they reach us first, I wonder in which country it would be the best for them to land?

> **R. Leven**
> Chalfont St Peter, Buckinghamshire

LOONY TUNES

SIR – Now that we've decided cartoons have the right to cause mild offence and we're all 'Charlie', please can we have Tom and Jerry back on television?

G.L.
Aylesbury, Buckinghamshire

SIR – Over the past few days I have cried on several occasions while watching television. From Wednesday to Friday I cried in despair at the unfolding events in Paris. The barbarity and cruelty of Islamic extremists were difficult to come to terms with.

On Saturday I cried as I watched the *Mamma Mia!* movie on ITV. I grew up (sort of, although I don't really believe that I have grown up) in the 1970s and 1980s and I loved ABBA and their music. Part of my caring soul was reborn, after the death of my belief in humanity during the previous three days.

I am 68 years old and life will go on, for the time being.

Peter Ellis,
Grewelthorpe, North Yorkshire

SIR – In a normal week *Charlie Hebdo* is seen by 0.05 per cent of the population of France. The first issue after the killings was seen by at least 0.1 per cent of the population of the planet. Why did the killers bother?

Ken Nicholson
Glasgow

SIR – Last week we cried, 'Je suis Charlie'. This week the lid was put firmly on to prevent publication of the Chilcot Report. Just where do we stand on free speech?

Barry Bond
Leigh-on-Sea, Essex

THE DOG ATE MY CHILCOT

SIR – Now that the Chilcot Inquiry has become something of a national joke surely it is only a matter of time before 'doing a Chilcot' passes into common useage for anything that is severely or inexplicably delayed. For example, one might say, 'My builder has done a Chilcot on the loft conversion', or 'I'm sorry, Sir, I've done a bit of a Chilcot with my maths homework'.

The possibilities are as endless as the Inquiry.

Martyn Thomas
London SE27

SIR – The other day my wife and I were talking about celebrating my 60th birthday next year. She asked me what I'd like to live to see, supposing I reached 90.

I replied, 'The publication of the Chilcot Report.'

Do you think this is a reasonable hope for me to cherish?

Bob Timmis
Warrington, Cheshire

SIR – Which will come first, Grexit or Chilcot?

G. Smith
Marlow, Buckinghamshire

INNOVATIVE GREEK BAILOUTS

SIR – I'm surprised that nobody has made the obvious suggestion for alleviating the Greek financial situation, namely that we should buy the Parthenon for a billion pounds or so. It would look very fine on Hampstead Heath, and I believe the British Museum has some appropriate sculptures that might fit it.

Of course, this would also provide a solution to a long-running dispute.

David Fletcher
High Wycombe, Buckinghamshire

SIR – The Greek crisis rumbles on. Perhaps
if someone had the courage to ask the Duke of
Edinburgh his opinion on this crisis, he would tell
them to just f****** get on with it.

Neil Green
South Newbald, East Yorkshire

SIR – Greece is facing serious problems in
reducing her debts. At the same time, illegal
immigrants are entering the EU by paddling from
Turkey to Kos, which Greece (and others) would
like to stop.

An onlooker might suggest that Greece sell Kos
to Turkey.

Martin Smith
Brimpsfield, Gloucestershire

SIR – Greece and other indebted nations might
do well to heed the wisdom found in the book of
Proverbs – the borrower is a slave to the lender.
There is nothing new under the sun.

Jeremy Eves
Bangor, Co Down

SIR – I took over the household finances following
a vote of confidence from my wife and young
daughter. I immediately phoned my bank to tell
them that I was not going to pay my loan repayments
for the foreseeable future. Would they actually

consider writing off the debt? To my surprise, they said, 'Yes, no problem; we get asked this all the time and by the way, would you like a gift of more money as you don't seem to be very good at living within your means?'

Then I woke up from my dream.

Jonathan Elderton
Cambridge

SIR – Why does the European Union seem to love Greece despite its fecklessness, and despise Great Britain? The parable of the Prodigal Son comes to mind.

Graham Bond
Matching Green, Essex

SIR – I am convinced that democracy is breaking out in Brussels. It's four days now since the Greek elections and Brussels has not asked the Greeks to try again for the correct answer.

Stephen Thackray
Mollington, Cheshire

SIR – To reward his negotiating skills, will the Greek Finance Minister now afford himself a necktie?

Andrew Grey
Kingswood, Surrey

SIR – If the Greeks are not going to have a *Grexit*, are they going to have a *Grin*?

Margaret Senior
Uppingham, Rutland

SIR – Would you please instruct your financial journalists to desist from using the dreadful terms *Brexit* and *Grexit*. Otherwise I may be forced into a *Telegrexit*, which would leave me utterly bereaved.

Ted Shorter
Hildenborough, Kent

SIR – You report that 'Putin could ride to the rescue of Greece'. Surely this is simply another attempt by Russia to gain warm water ports, a policy she has had for 200 years?

Robin Nonhebel
Swanage, Dorset

SIR – Given Syriza's blatant procrastination, obfuscation, bad faith, brinkmanship, ambiguous affection for President Putin and invisible diplomatic skills, it is abundantly clear that Greece is simply taking the Michaelides.

Charles Foster
Chalfont St Peter, Buckinghamshire

OUR MAN IN HIS ARMCHAIR

SIR – Merkel and Hollande have the chance to kill two birds with one stone: Persuade Putin to withdraw from the Ukraine, in return for which he can annexe Greece unopposed.

This diplomacy lark is a doddle.

David S. Sandhurst
Chaffcombe, Somerset

SIR – You report that RAF Typhoon fighters were recently scrambled to intercept Russian bombers flying off the coast of Bournemouth. As a result, the Russian Ambassador was summoned to explain the reasons for the incident. We often hear of ambassadors being summoned, but we are never told what their explanations were.

Michael Cattell
Mollington, Cheshire

SIR – You report that an assassination attempt on Mr Putin was foiled by Scotland Yard.

Why?

David Money
Cambridge

SIR – You recently reported that Ed Miliband
shared an intimate dinner with George Clooney and
his wife, but then went on to explain that this was a
business dinner attended by several people to discuss
sanctions against Russia.

This sounds about as intimate as mowing the
lawn.

Clive Pilley
Westcliff-on-Sea, Essex

1815 AND ALL THAT

SIR – I note some reported reticence by the
French to join in wholeheartedly with our victory
celebrations for the Battle of Waterloo. Is this
so surprising? I wonder how we will feel if the
French decide to promote the 1,000th anniversary
celebrations in 2066 in Britain for their victory at
the Battle of Hastings.

Michael G. Handcock
Cookham, Berkshire

SIR – The Battle of Waterloo lasted from 7a.m.
until 5p.m. on one day 200 years ago. The re-
enactment is set to last two days. Who says there isn't
inflation?

Flo Kaufmann
London N2

SIR – Surely the best way to commemorate the sealing of the Magna Carta would be for the government to relinquish its powers and place them back into the hands of the monarch?

Jack Caprani
Hornsea, East Yorkshire

ENGLISH INDEPENDENCE DAY

SIR – My wife and I were living in the Far East in the 1960s. Each Fourth of July the American Ambassador would hold a mammoth party.

Shaking his hand in the reception line, I remarked that it was a great day for the United States and that I was so glad that we had won.

A little later a 6' 6" US Marine appeared at my elbow and said, 'Suh, the Ambassador would like a word, Suh.'

The Ambassador said, 'You were glad that we won, but you're English?'

'Yes,' I replied. 'It was a fight between English settlers and a German King, and the English won.'

With a big smile he said, 'Well, that's one way of looking at it.'

Keith Chadbourn
Over Compton, Dorset

MARY, QUEEN OF CALAIS

SIR – If Queen Mary I thought Calais would be written across her heart when she died some 450 years ago, she will undoubtedly be turning in her grave at the recent events there and the effect upon our country.

Nicholas Faulkner
Romsey, Hampshire

SIR – June 1940, there are thousands of German soldiers waiting in Calais to invade Britain.

June 2015, there are 3,000 illegal immigrants waiting in Calais to invade Britain. Will we have to fight them on the beaches?

Tony Luker
Chineham, Hampshire

ANARCHY IN EUROPE DAY

SIR – VE Day in Athens was sunny and warm. The Military Police were cruising the streets collecting drunks and laying them out peacefully in marquees that had been erected in Zappeion Gardens.

Outside the Eden Hotel, which the RAF were using, Big Jock the Glaswegian wireless operator was painting 'Joe Stalin for King' in two-foot letters across the road.

A young pilot who was duty officer for the day came up and said, 'Really, airman, I know it's VE Day, but you're going too far.'

Jock said, 'If ye dinna clear off I'll paint ya knees.'

The officer said, 'You can't speak to me like that.'

Jock said, 'Too late' and painted his knees.

The officer, at a loss, walked away.

Keith Herdman
Whitley Bay, Northumberland

SIR – On the evening before VE Day 1948 I remember watching senior boys at my boarding school in Kent building a bonfire for the celebrations next day. As I looked across the playing fields to the orchards over which I had watched Spitfires and Tempests shooting down flying bombs, I was filled with a terrible sadness. Despite all the deprivations and the dangers which the war had brought, I knew that I would never see such great days again.

M.G.
Tonbridge, Kent

SIR – What a remarkable contrast in VE Day anniversary celebrations. In London, an open-air concert with nostalgic songs, emotional readings and the audience singing and dancing in the aisles: a united knees-up.

In Moscow, a dour parade of thousands of marching armed troops, missiles and tanks.

Geoff Jones
Ross-on-Wye, Herefordshire

SAINT NICHOLAS

SIR – My wife and I were enjoying lunch on our cruise when an elderly gentleman made his way with some difficulty to our table. He looked at my plate and said, 'I see you have soused herrings. I wish I'd seen them, as my wife used to prepare them for me.'

When I offered to go and get some for him, he said, 'Why should you do that for me?'

It was only later that we found out that the elderly gentleman was Sir Nicholas Winton. We were struck by the humility he had shown in response to my very minor courtesy once we knew what he had done for so many.

Peter Freeman
Little Hale, Lincolnshire

TOPLESS TRADITIONS

SIR – In Sarawak (Borneo), just after the war, young ladies were topless all the time. When I was there in

1965, on secondment to the Malaysian Army, it was only the very elderly who continued the habit.

In 1945 I was in Batavia (now Jakarta) and, in a main street at a large water tub, there was a young lady washing herself topless. She wore a sarong from the waist down.

If Eleanor Hawkins was topless on Mount Kinabalu (and not naked as in some reports), I suggest she was just carrying on an old tradition.

Leonard Chandler
Rushmere St Andrew, Suffolk

SIR – When Eleanor Hawkins decided to strip on a Malaysian mountain more than her physical attributes were on show. She was displaying her upbringing, education and morals, in short a British way of life. Pure class!

Peter Corke
Ivybridge, Devon

THE GREAT IRISH BAKE-OFF

SIR – Unnecessary litigation might have been avoided if the baker and customer in Northern Ireland had explained to each other their respective views on gay marriage and looked for a satisfactory compromise.

For instance, the baker could have offered to

produce a cake with the words, 'We do not support gay marriage' in such a way that the first three words could be easily removed by the purchaser.

David Lockwood
Worksop, Nottinghamshire

SIR – When next in Northern Ireland will I be within my rights to enter a Jewish deli and demand they make me a bacon sandwich?

Robert Langford
Keresley, West Midlands

SIR – I have my own business. Please can someone advise me if it is now illegal to turn down work.

Victoria Buckingham
Hallaton, Leicestershire

SIR – Now that we have seen the successful attempt by a powerful lobby to weaponise the baking industry, will *The Great British Bake Off* introduce a new category of 'the cake that causes the greatest offence'?

Jean Edwards
Newhey, Lancashire

PRISON BREAK

SIR – Captain Schettino, the Captain of the ill-fated *Costa Concordia*, has been jailed for 16 years and (with immediate effect) banned from commanding a vessel for five years. How very Italian. I didn't realise they had prison ships.

Sandy Pratt
Dormansland, Surrey

PROTESTANT INDULGENCE

SIR – The Pope has announced it is acceptable to smack naughty children. As a Protestant, do I have to wait for permission from the Archbishop of Canterbury or may I begin immediately?

Glenys Baylis
Abberton, Worcestershire

SIR – The Pope may or may not be right about climate change, but he should focus his readers closer to home. For instance, churches with under-pew heating should only heat the front four rows, so that the elderly and infirm can occupy them, while the rest of us should be encouraged to wear more clothes.

I would also recommend banning Formula One, and repealing the Hunting Act, as hunting is a much more eco-friendly activity than jetting off to a beach somewhere.

Adair Anderson
Selkirk

BORN IN THE USA

SIR – A few years ago my wife, who is Peruvian, was visiting a small village in the Peruvian countryside. She came across a pretty little village girl and asked her name.

Madinusa was the reply.

'That's an unusual name,' said my wife. 'How did your mother select that?'

The little girl replied that it was on a tin of peaches.

David Hodges
Ickham, Kent

SIR – We gave our son the name John, thinking that it could never be shortened. I was therefore somewhat surprised, while walking through Broadgate with him some years ago, when he answered to a loud greeting, 'Hi, Tits'.

Margaret Oates
Ditcham, Hampshire

THE USE AND
ABUSE OF
LANGUAGE

FRUITY SIGNS

SIR – A number of years ago, in a hotel in Padalarang in Java, I spotted signs on every room door that firmly stated in three languages, Indonesian, Dutch and English: 'No whores or durian fruit permitted in this room'.

Simon Edsor
London SW1

SIR – Some years ago, staying at the St James Hotel in Barbados, I was amused to read a notice inviting guests to enjoy themselves in Tara's Brassiere.

I did not avail myself of the pleasure.

Alan Shaw
Halifax

SIR – At a bar in Mahon: 'Try our sangria. You will never get better'.

Dr John Mitchell
Potters Bar, Hertfordshire

SIR – A local five-star hotel's cocktail menu had an unappetising drink including the ingredient: 'A sh*t of lime'.

David Gambling
Hemel Hempstead, Hertfordshire

SIR – The recent correspondence about misnaming and misspelling of foodstuffs reminds me of the hilarious sign in a shop window in Wallsend when we were conducting a site inspection of a parade of shops prior to a planning inquiry in that town.

An unfortunate fishmonger had chalked up on the inside of his window: 'Fresh crap 50p a pot'.

Not even the freshness of the ingredients would induce us to enter.

Richard Phillips QC
London EC4

SIR – On the notice board of the Allerford Reading Rooms, West Somerset: 'Saturday 14th Feb: Fish and Chip van in car park. Skittles after'.

Can there be a more romantic St. Valentine's evening?

Andre Baker
Minehead, Somerset

SIR – I stopped holidaying in Cornwall many years ago. It was not only the restrictive access to beaches but the aggressive signs installed by local councils which made us, as dog owners, unwelcome.

Fortunately, other parts of the UK have a more pro-active approach. In Wales it is not uncommon to find beaches where signs indicate, 'Dogs left' and 'People right'.

I have yet to find a beach with the third option of: 'Children straight on'.

K.R.
Monmouth

TYRELESS PEDANTS

SIR – I very much doubt that your correspondent who reported that 'One third of drivers cannot change a tyre' has ever tried himself. It is much more usual – and easier – to change the wheel.

Richard Glover
Edinburgh

SIR – Recently in a pub I ordered a baguette, asking if I could have it without the apostrophe. They didn't get the point.

Tony Greenham
Sutton, Cheshire

SIR – I always avoid filling in tick-box questionnaires. However, if there is an opportunity, I point out that being satisfied can be compared to being pregnant, in that either one is or isn't, not 'very' or 'less than'.

Den Beves
Pennant, Powys

SIR – My wife buys extra virgin olive oil. I am at a loss as to what this actually is. Extra virgin strikes me as the polar opposite of a wee bit pregnant. Both conditions strike me as implausible. Am I missing something?

David Brown
Lavenham, Suffolk

SIR – Eddie Redmayne playing Stephen Hawking in *The Theory of Everything* prefaces his order in a Cambridge bar in the 1960s with 'Can I get . . .' This unfortunate expression is very much a 21st-century invention.

Mike Francis
Bierton, Buckinghamshire

I AM NOT BRIDISH

SIR – A true Brit would never use Americanisms. 'Gonna', the favourite word of George Osborne, is a no-no. Replacing the letter 't' with the letter 'd' is a no-no-no-no. I am *British*. I am not *Bridish*.

I am not going to sit here and accept the Americanisation of our language. Do you *geddit* or do you get it? It is insidious and needs to be stopped by the Broadcasting Watchdog.

Phil Wall
Cassagne, Haute Garonne, France

SIR – I was horrified to see that *sulphur* may now be spelled *sulfur*. If we continue to Americanise the English language I hate to think what they may make of *phosphorus*.

John Ledger
Munster, Ireland

WEASEL WORDS

SIR – It doesn't matter what weasel words are used to deceive us that the NHS is 'free at the point of use' or 'free at the point of access' or 'free at the point of entry'; it remains nonsense. When I turn on a light I am not required to pay at that moment, but the electricity is not free then, or at any time.

Martin Burgess
Beckenham, Kent

SIR – How many times do we hear politicians – most recently David Cameron in a television interview – deflect questions with the statement: 'If you're asking me . . .'?

Isn't it time the interviewers responded with a firm: 'I'm not asking you that'?

Christopher Boyle
Milton Keynes, Buckinghamshire

SIR – While listening to members of the Australian cricket team being interviewed on radio, I noticed most of them started their responses with a superfluous 'Yeah, no', or 'No, yeah'. Please can someone tell them to stop this affectation. It is nearly as irritating as the rising inflection many Aussies insert into their sentences, which has the effect of making every statement into a question.

Parminder Summon
Peterborough, Cambridgeshire

SIR – Why does there seem to be a vogue for prefixing verbs with 'pre'? We are always invited to 'pre-order' products (I am happy just to order them) and today I read of a journalist 'pre-taping' (yes, taping) an interview.

I also regularly hear of reports being pre-recorded. How does that work and what is the difference when it comes to the final recording?

Jeremy C.N. Price
Cromarty, Ross and Cromarty

MEDIA VICES

SIR – Your political correspondent describes Michael Dugher MP as 'Labour's vice chair'. Steady on! I always thought a vice chair was an item of kinky furniture, usually to be found in a (cough) massage parlour.

I wonder when *Telegraph* writers will observe the style guide. Or when a kind subeditor will spare us from this constipated left-wing language.

G.M.
Edinburgh

SIR – In my *Daily Telegraph* there is a report of an 'assualt' [sic] at Aintree. Are you now employing ex *Guardian* workers?

John Anderson
Dublin

SIR – I was astonished to read in one of your recent leader articles your reference to someone 'being bested'. As far as I am aware there is no such verb in the English language.

S.T.
East Keswick, West Yorkshire

SIR – Does Boris Johnson prepare his weekly rants using a Scrabble board? I can see no other explanation for his use of the word *convoke* on Monday. I hope he managed to get the K on a triple-letter square.

Clive Pilley
Westcliff-on-Sea, Essex

SIR – Please could the editor explain what he means by 'extra-martial sex'?

Dr Wendy Roles
Sunningdale, Berkshire

SIR – I am beginning to worry about the *Telegraph's* use of the English language. Recently in your racing column there was reference to someone's 'spinal chord'. (Could that possibly be the lost chord musicians have been searching for?)

Now I see that Lord and Lady Long's home on top of Towan Island is 'one of the most unique' addresses in the country.

Judith Payne
Low Cocklaw, Northumberland

SIR – Yet again I note an adjective in the wrong place: 'Lightweight men's summer trousers'.

R.M. Daughton
Cardiff

SIR – For this anniversary year of 2015 I have two ambitions: to see all four Great Charters and to have it generally accepted that Magna Carta was sealed at Runnymede.

As an erstwhile History teacher I am happy to offer my services, unpaid, as a proof reader for your newspaper, in order that your reporters may avoid any more references to the signing of Magna Carta.

Mary Moore
Croydon, Surrey

SIR – Allister Heath is guilty of using the same short-sighted inflationary nomenclature which he decries in successive governments when they re-named vocational training certificates as 'degrees'.

He describes retail sales, hamburger flipping, labouring and van driving as 'professions'.

What shall we now call brain surgery? Yet another service industry?

Pete Townsend
Bristol

SIR – Would Bryony Gordon please stop writing 'we' this and 'we' that. She may think that everyone agrees with her opinion on everything, but she needs to be disabused of this.

Maurice Hastings
Bickington, Devon

SIR – How long has it been acceptable to begin a sentence with a conjunction? Almost daily on Radio 4's *Today* programme interviewees begin to answer a question with the word *so*.

Have the rules been changed without anyone telling me? Or is this another nail in the coffin of the English language?

G.P.F.
Stock Green, Worcestershire

SIR – Tonight we have been told by the BBC that 'people arrived in a number of vehicles dressed as policemen'. It is this sort of drivel which is inducing our children to mangle our language.

Robert Rodrigo
Burwell, Cambridgeshire

SIR – The BBC wishes to recruit weather presenters who don't need to be experts in meteorology but should be disabled. I'd be quite happy if they could find someone who can correctly pronounce the word *particularly*.

Geoff Deighton
Old Tupton, Derbyshire

WHAT TO CALL ISIS

SIR – Wouldn't a more fitting name for the Middle Eastern thugs be BANDILs (Bandits of Iraq and the Lebanon)?

Roderick Taylor
Abbotsbrook, Buckinghamshire

SIR – As well as debating what the BBC should call ISIS/ISIL, can we dispense with the meaningless word *radicalisation*? This sounds more like machinations within the Labour Party than what it really means: an invitation to confused people to take part in rape, torture, mass killing and the destruction of heritage.

If we must have an abstract polysyllable – no doubt so that those who debate the issues can sound well-informed and grown up – how about *fanaticisation*?

Similarly with *Jihadi*. I have no interest in their assumed motivation; *terrorist* works for me.

Philip Brennan
Oxhill, Warwickshire

SIR – There was I thinking that the BBC's *W1A* was a parody of the BBC – it would appear that it was a documentary.

Alan Russell
Dibden Purlieu, Hampshire

SIR – Behind this so-called Islamic State you will find various people including 'Tony' Blair and Cherie Booth.

Who may well have converted to something called Islam.

'Tony' is a 22 SAS 'Lead Scout'

Or 'LS'

And: 'It is Tony and me'

I and I.

Or I + I.

Therefore: 'L + S + I + I' = 'I + S + I + L'.

Geddit?

Proles.

The British Media KNOW this.

'People' like Andrew Neil.

But try and hide it by saying IS, not ISIL.

There you go.

M

DIRECTOR, MI5

cc The Robots

M, Director, MI5 ('On Holiday')

The Royal Navy 'Trident' Submarines

MI7

MOD

CIA

The Vatican

The United Nations

INDIGESTABLE PUNS

SIR – I don't wish to make a meal of it, but I have an ongoing beef with this election. With all its sturgeons, salmonds, and kippers, it is hardly sporting of the politicians continually to duck key issues in the ham-fisted and sheepish manner illustrated in this evening's television debate.

Dr Bertie Dockerill
Shildon, Co Durham

SIR – According to Fiona Bruce, George Osborne has moved to *Darning* Street. Is this so he can be nearer the old woman on Threadneedle Street?

Les Stoker
Fairburn, West Yorkshire

SIR – You report that the good ladies of Chipping Ongar are upset that their heritage railway has been used to film unsavoury scenes and they fear that their children may be polluted. Have they never enjoyed the ritual of mating in the back of a taxi? Do they want cabbies to show a certificate of moral cleanliness? A bit Uber the top, don't you think?

Tony Jones
London SW7

SIR – I don't know much about golf but I would have thought the least that exponents could do is clean their balls in the privacy of the rough.

David Brown
Lavenham, Suffolk

SIR – As a result of her colourful language in support of her fiancé Andy Murray at the Australian Open might Kim Sears henceforth be known as Kim Swears?

Lesley Thompson
Lavenham, Suffolk

SIR – It was no surprise to me that England were beaten by Bangladesh in the cricket World Cup. I've always said that if you eat Bangladeshi curry you can get the runs.

Neville Landau
London SW19

SPORTING
TRIUMPH AND
DISASTER

STRENUOUS ARMCHAIR SPORTS

SIR – My wife would like to thank the judiciary for declaring bridge to be a sport because she can now say with hand on heart that she does four hours sport per week.

Perhaps they would like to consider the strenuous art of raising a glass, too?

Richard Waldron
Woolavington, Somerset

SIR – Your correspondents conclude that qualification for an activity to acquire the status of a sport requires that the participants have to change their footwear.

Can I count myself as a sportsman when labouring in my vegetable garden?

Michael Cole
Edington, Somerset

SIR – I use the following simple methodology: does the participant perspire as a result of their exertions?

Paul Codrington
Minster-on-Sea, Kent

SIR – Your leading article asks which of darts, croquet, chess, shooting and bridge is not a sport. Of these only shooting is a sport, and then only if it is game shooting. The others are games, though some would describe chess and bridge as pastimes.

Alasdair Ogilvy
Stedham, West Sussex

TRYING RUGBY BEHAVIOUR

SIR – When I was involved in rugby trophy ceremonies (admittedly some years ago now), we did not jump up and down on the spot like demented jacks in the box. Nor did we spray our clothing with perfectly drinkable champagne.

While the standard of rugby played by Ireland throughout the Six Nations Tournament is to be applauded, the childish, boorish display by the Irish players at the presentation ceremony is not. I have witnessed more adult-like behaviour at my grandson's nursery school.

You may forward this letter to the Irish Rugby Football Union if you choose.

Colonel S.O. Thomas (retd)
Ogmore by Sea, Glamorgan

SIR – In my rugby playing days the final whistle signified the end of proceedings and both teams and the referee retired to the bar for a beer or two.

Nowadays, sadly, this is no longer the case as

the men in anoraks emerge after the match and start looking for an incident they can use to cite somebody. This drags on through disciplinary panels and appeals and a single game becomes an ongoing drama.

Is it really necessary and what has changed?

Commodore C.M.J. Carson
Budleigh Salterton, Devon

BLATTER THE BOUNDER

SIR – Sepp Blatter cannot be both a cad and a bounder, as your correspondent suggests. I was taught that a cad is one who knows the rules and chooses not to play by them, whereas a bounder is one who has no training in etiquette protocols.

Even a cad wouldn't wear brown shoes with a dark suit; this Blatter fellow is clearly a bounder.

Andrew Wands
Canisbay, Caithness

SIR – Sepp Blatter is to good football governance what Tony Blair, Middle East peace envoy, is to peace.

Tim Coles
Carlton, Bedfordshire

SIR – The news of Tony Blair resigning from his peace envoy role makes me wonder if he fancies taking on FIFA.

Peter Ballantyne
Cowbridge, Glamorgan

SIR – The press has been buzzing with news of an enormous, unaccountable, multinational organisation that is characterised by over 20 years of 'rampant, systemic and deep-rooted' corruption. Are they talking about FIFA or the EU?

Louis Altman
London SW17

SIR – The word *blat* is widely used in Russian and describes one of the pillars of the Russian way of life. It is akin to nepotism, only with *blat* no blood ties are necessary for one party to bestow favours upon another.

The origins of the word go back to the beginning of the 20th century, to the Ukrainian city of Odessa and its underworld of Jewish gangs. 'Blat' meant 'initiated, privy to', in Yiddish jargon.

Tony Cox
Redhill, Surrey

SIR – I see that FIFA have suspended the bidding process for the 2026 World Cup.

Presumably all bribes already paid will be reimbursed?

Peter Fayers
Cape Town, South Africa

SIR – To avoid further upsets perhaps FIFA might consider adopting the same strategy as the Eurovision Song Contest where the following event is held in the previous winner's country?

Sarah Gall
Rochdale, Lancashire

SIR – May I suggest a halfway house between competing in the next World Cup and boycotting it. Let us resolve to go there but make sure we do not progress past the group stage. I believe we took the same moral stance against FIFA corruption in the last World Cup.

Dr David Parkinson
Bowdon, Cheshire

SIR – I don't know why there is so much fuss about FIFA. It seems to me that they have the best officials money can buy.

Jeremy Bateman
Luton

SIR – So Sepp Blatter has been re-elected as FIFA President. He must feel like a million dollars.

Jonathan Batt
Castle Cary, Somerset

SIR – How long now before Mr Blatter develops amnesia?

Tony Fewell
Marlow, Buckinghamshire

SIR – I have decided that rather than have FIFA's machinations thrust at me during this wonderful weather, it would be far more interesting and productive to undercoat and topcoat every single piece of stone on my gravel drive.

Anthony Peter Bolton
Church Stretton, Shropshire

EARLY BATH AT THE OFFICE

SIR – If, on the rare occasions that I get something right at work, I celebrated by removing my shirt, my bosses would be less than impressed. My work colleagues (who clearly do not recognise an Adonis when they see one) have made it clear that they would demand

at least a red card. Why should football be any
different?

Clive Pilley
Westcliff-on-Sea, Essex

SIR – Is there a reason why professional footballers
are all photographed with their mouths open? Is
it a desire to show us the condition of their teeth
and tonsils? Or do they suffer from a breathing
malfunction which causes a frantic desire for oxygen
and flies?

Alison Adams
Trowbridge, Wiltshire

SIR – With today's report showing that one in
35 men is a potential paedophile why is the awful
custom of footballers coming onto the field
clutching a small boy's hand not stopped?

C.L.
London SE21

THE NEW COLEEN ROONEYS

SIR – With England doing so well in the women's
football World Cup, will there be a new TV series
called *Footballer's Husbands*?

Frank Tomlin
Billericay, Essex

SIR – The women's World Cup has proved that the constant spitting by male footballers is an unnecessary and disgusting habit. I wonder if the men habitually spit on their carpets at home?

Brian Rushton
Stourport-on-Severn, Worcestershire

SIR – Your readers who failed to stay up to watch our ladies' football team play Norway on Monday missed not only an exhibition of excellent female talent and a brilliant victory, but also a line from the commentator to outdo the recent apparently contentious statement of Sir Tim Hunt.

After an incident on the field the commentator remarked that if the player were sent off 'they would be down to ten men'.

Professor Roy Pike
Malvern, Worcestershire.

PUTT UP AND SHUT UP

SIR – Once more the Cabinet Members at my pub have met, this time to consider the case of Peter Alliss and the BBC's apology on his behalf.

His sin was to suggest that, while a professional golfer poised over a vital putt, the golfer's wife could well be thinking of the reward of a new kitchen.

After careful consideration, we have taken the following unanimous decision: Stop the World; we want to get off.

Allan Littlemore
Sandbach, Cheshire

SIR - My wife wonders: if Peter Alliss had said, 'She might get a new lawnmower', would that have been acceptable to the BBC?

Q. David Mcgill
Sutton Coldfield, West Midlands

CRICKET AND PEACE

SIR – I have long believed, perhaps erroneously, that we never make war against people whom we play at cricket. It is, therefore, most appropriate that we are playing Afghanistan in the World Cup on the very day on which we celebrate the end of our military involvement in their war-torn land.

Daphne Clarke
Richmond, North Yorkshire

SIR – Perhaps Bangladesh and Afghanistan should send their cricket teams to take on Syria, Iraq and other Middle East states. There is nothing like sport to sort out friction between various religions, races and tribes.

Roger Haines
Crowborough, East Sussex

SIR – I am mortified that Cheltenham Ladies' College is dispensing with prep. With students moaning about prep and the difficulty of exams, and public schools removing cricket from the curriculum, one worries about the future of the nation.

Mark Donkin
South Normanton, Derbyshire

SIR – Following the recent results of the English cricket team in the World Cup, may I suggest a duck as the national bird for England?

Gerry Gomez
Walsall, West Midlands

SIR – With England's latest humiliation fresh in mind, your readers may like to know that some years ago, in a pre-World Cup warm-up game in Worcester, The Lamb and Flag Cricket Club, in a 60-over match, gave the then Bangladesh side a respectable run for their money.

Nevill Swanson
Worcester

FUNKY FIELD PLACINGS

SIR — I love cricket. I love the brilliant commentary and analysis on BBC radio and Sky TV. However, the next time I hear the word 'funky' in relation to field placings I swear I won't be accountable for my actions. Can't they find a better adjective?

Nicholas Dear
Wombourne, Staffordshire

SIR — As a cricket fan I have over the years learned to cope with the constant reiterations of the words *pressure* and *equation* which are beaten ruthlessly to death on a daily basis by Messrs Gower, Atherton, Botham, Hussain and Lloyd.

I can even cope with Hussain's 'he was sat' and the 'genuine edge' so favoured by Sir Ian Botham — to distinguish it from the false, bogus or facsimile edges with which cricket is so richly favoured.

However, after 200 years of *batsmen* this group of commentators have now decided to substitute it with *batters*. This is a step too far.

N.S. Nash
Malmesbury, Wiltshire

SIR — It was unfortunate that my sister's annual visit to inspect my home coincided with the final One Day International, England versus New Zealand.

Her knowledge of all sports, like her interest in them, is just about zero.

Realising that it was boiling up to a tense finish I switched on my radio to hear the closing overs. With each roar of the crowd to mark a boundary or a wicket she cried out, 'Who's winnin'?'

Just how does one answer such a question?

Richard Holroyd
Cambridge

SIR – When I (rarely) watch football on television I'm used to them kissing and hugging each other, but I was horrified while watching the cricket World Cup last weekend in Australia. England cricketers, yes, cricketers, patted each other on the bum at every opportunity.

Speechless. I'm running out of sports.

James Rolls
Petworth, West Sussex

SIR – There can be no doubt that our England cricket captain's run of very poor scores is down to his picking the wrong strokes to play at the given time. However, this could not be said of his nose-picking habit, which rates up there with the best of them.

Fielding as he does in the slips, this is invariably caught by the cameras. Unless he can eschew this rather distasteful habit, I suggest he takes up a position somewhere in the outfield, where he can indulge to his heart's content.

John D. Berman
New Barnet, Hertfordshire

SIR – As W.G. Grace said about the introduction of professional cricketers: 'Betting and all kindred evils will follow in its wake, and instead of the game being followed up for love, it will simply be a matter of £ s d.'

Like MPs, it was better when they were not paid but did it for their country.

Anthony Cardew
London W1

WE NEED TO TALK ABOUT KEVIN

SIR – Never mind Europe, David Cameron must call an early referendum on the issue that is really seizing the national debate. Should Kevin Pietersen be picked for the England cricket team or not?

Keith Flett
London N17

SIR – If ever two people deserved each other, it must be Piers Morgan and Kevin Pietersen.

John Harries
Estepona, Spain

SIR – I would like to apply for the job of England's Director of Cricket. I loathe cricket with a passion and do not really know much about the game but I have been a cricket widow for the past 30 years. As a wife and mother of a grown-up son, I am totally capable of dealing with all these boys.

Fiona Reynolds
Redhill, Surrey

SIR – Perhaps one of the wider questions on the Kevin Pietersen affair has yet to be answered: how was Andrew Strauss able to enter the Lord's Pavilion without wearing a jacket and tie? As an MCC member I would like to know how he did it.

Chris Florence
Walton-on-Thames, Surrey

SIR – Having just bought himself a house in Sunningdale, if Kevin Pietersen is looking for a job this coming winter perhaps he could come and turn on our Christmas lights.

Duncan Rayner
Sunningdale, Berkshire

RIP, RICHIE BENAUD

SIR – In the early 1970s, as a trainee solicitor, I was asked by a partner to take up references for a prospective tenant who wished to rent a client's flat for the summer. On discovering that the tenant was one Richard Benaud I informed my superior that references would not be required and, if necessary, I would vouch for the tenant. I was told not to be so silly and get on and do it, which I reluctantly did.

I remained convinced, however, that this was totally unnecessary and feel vindicated by Richie's family being offered a state funeral.

Brian Freedman
Hove, East Sussex

SIR –

The voice of my youth is now gone.
Stumps have been drawn on his ultimate game.
The team is diminished by one.
The scorer has scored a black line through his name.

He is in the pavilion with Packer,
That voice of the summer and summer's rewards,
As dry as the wicket at WACA,
As mellow and clipped as the outfield at Lord's.

Old Father Time has called Time,
Has bowled him a beamer and battered his box.
So now shall the Passing bell chime
For the buttery blazer and silvery Locks.

The light of our summers is out,

Only just 16 short of his century.
Oh, how much; (let nobody doubt)
That mellifluous 'marvellous' meant to me.

Now the Spinner has Got 'im! at last;
Bowled into the footmarks and gone round his legs.
As he himself did in the past,
Has spun him some dreamtime and rattled the pegs.

There's a witty Bordeaux in the fridge,
So turn on the wireless and raise up a glass.
Let us catch the last hour from Trent Bridge
And dwell on the Memories now under grass.

For Life like the summer is short
And long are the shadows at Close of Play,
So every run must be bought
And wickets should never be given away.

But all in the end are undone,
No matter the batter, the innings he's had;
The bouncer full out of the sun,
The edge to the Keeper, the rap on the pad.

Oh, the blaze of the sun on the nape
Of a neck that is gnarled and the colour of rust;
From Chester le Street to the Cape
Ashes are Ashes, and all is now dust.

      T.D.P.

LAND OF OTHER PEOPLE'S
FATHERS

SIR – Can somebody tell us why, when a country
called England plays a vital Ashes match against a
country called Australia, the contest takes place in a
country called Wales?

Anthony Turl
London SW1

SIR – Why are so many Welshmen wearing yellow
hats at Cardiff this weekend?

Andrew Smith
Epping, Essex

SIR – I am sitting by a swimming pool in Crete,
trying simultaneously to keep the Greek economy
afloat and to listen to England's cricketing progress
in Cardiff.

Unfortunately I am doing neither. It looks as
though Comrade Putin has a wallet larger than
mine, and the shambles that is the BBC would
be better suited to running a circus than a
broadcasting service.

What it terms 'rights issues' are preventing me
from listening to *Test Match Special* from my iPad. Yet
these are intermittent. On Wednesday I was not able
to listen to anything, but on Thursday there was
uninterrupted coverage of Joe Root smashing the

blighters to all parts of Cardiff. Today, I am again prevented from following the action.

Is there no one at the BBC who is competent?

Nicholas Sherriff
London SW11

SIR – I think someone should check the width of the Australians' bats. They look far wider than ours.

David Slater
Flimwell, East Sussex

SIR – In the wake of the ghastly performance by the English cricket team in the Lord's Test, let us take heart from the performance of the style consultants to the team who ensured that the correct combinations of caps, sunglasses and chewing gum were always in evidence at the appropriate times.

Patrick Thomas
Over Wallop, Hampshire

SIR – After Australia's batting performance in the first innings of the fourth Ashes Test might we see their batsmen in the future punching the air and taking off their helmets to acknowledge spectators' applause on their scoring ten runs, instead of the customary fifty?

A.B. Kench
Navata, Spain

SIR – Congratulations to the England cricket team on regaining the Ashes, winning the last two Tests well within the allotted time. Does this mean that they are giving up playing on Sundays, thus opposing the Government's plans to relax the trading laws south of the border?

Revd E. Peter Mosley
Inverness

SIR – How on earth did England manage it without the help of that self-effacing team player from South Africa?

Guy Newman
Chalfont St Giles, Buckinghamshire

LOVE ALL, MURRAY

SIR – Your article criticised Kim Sears's wedding attire as 'old-fashioned'. Why is such scrutiny always reserved for the bride? I was disappointed there was no critique of Andy Murray's skirt of curtain material, leather bag with tassels, crumpled tie, square buttons, funereal socks and bladed weapon.

Peter Saunders
Salisbury, Wiltshire

SIR — I note the recent publicity given to Andy Murray's wedding. May I inform you that I, also, am happily married.

Malcolm Freeth
Bournemouth, Dorset

SIR — Some people take great delight in heralding spring with sightings of snowdrops, bluebells, swallows and cuckoos. I, on the other hand, prepare for battle with the insect world.

The season has now opened on my great mortal enemy: the buzzing bluebottle. My backhand using a folded *Daily Telegraph* has improved no end and, as Wimbledon approaches, it would have Andy Murray absolutely green with envy.

Geoff Milburn
Glossop, Derbyshire

WIMBLEDON WONDERINGS

SIR — Without being too indelicate, can somebody please enlighten me as to where the women competitors at Wimbledon put their spare balls?

With men, I can see that they go into a conventional pocket, but do the women have a reverse pocket within their skirts? Or do they rely on a piece of white knicker elastic to do the job?

Also, do the cries of ecstasy emitted during a shot have any bearing on the position of the spare ball?

John Holland
Dovercourt, Essex

SIR – Is there a connection between the glorious weather we've been enjoying this year and the absence of Cliff Richard?

Gordon Macniven
London SW17

SIR – When the players started grunting during Wimbledon I thought I couldn't possibly be more annoyed. Now the Australian fans have arrived.

Jane Cullinan
Padstow, Cornwall

SIR – I'm over the grunting and have moved on to the constant high-fives of the doubles players. Such a waste of energy.

David MacMillan
Bourne End, Buckinghamshire

SIR – Can the absurd, recently introduced practice of clapping, slowly and increasing in speed, when a player challenges an umpire's decision not be stopped? And can somebody who indulges in the practice tell me why?

Candy Haley
Cobham, Surrey

SIR – I await with bated breath the moment when the politically correct brigade lobby Wimbledon to suggest that the calling of 'fault' when a serve misses its mark is too negative and should be replaced by 'almost' to avoid the player's self-esteem being dented.

Chris Rice
Leominster, Herefordshire

SIR – Can anyone tell me why it was reported that Murray 'crashed out' of Wimbledon? What is the derivation of this phrase?

Jill Parry
Gosport, Hampshire

SIR – Why are men's tennis matches that go the distance always described as five-set thrillers and women's matches that go the distance never described as three-set thrillers?

W.G. McLellan
Collingtree, Northamptonshire

SIR – Does the constant repetition of 'Come on!' from the player's box actually help? Aren't they already trying?

Alan Mooge
Enfield, Middlesex

SIR – Why is John Motson able on his own to commentate on a football game that has 22 players, but tennis has to have more commentators than players (John McEnroe, John Lloyd and Andrew Castle on the Murray match)?

Bernard Bennett-Diver
Sanderstead, Surrey

SIR – In 1986, when there was still a standing area on Centre Court at Wimbledon, my friend and I queued overnight to watch Boris Becker in the Men's Final. During the evening a policeman passed on his way home and asked us what we would like for breakfast the following morning.

By morning we had been joined by hundreds of people who watched as the policeman walked up the road carrying a tray with two bacon rolls, coffees and orange juice and placed it on our laps.

He admitted his wife had cooked the bacon, as he wasn't very good at that sort of thing.

Jo Marchington
Ashtead, Surrey

SIR – Matt's cartoon today sums up my feelings about Wimbledon and the exploitation of children.

In the sports section was a photograph of a youngster holding an umbrella over a sweating tennis player. Had the player been engaged in combat? No, he had been chasing a little ball around a tennis court, prior to sitting down, wiping his brow with a towel (courtesy of the ball boy/girl), sipping a cold drink (courtesy of the ball boy/girl) and nibbling on a banana (courtesy of Mummy, perhaps).

If he gets too sweaty after resuming the chase of the little ball, back comes the ball boy/girl with a towel again.

We stopped sending children up chimneys over 100 years ago. Let these elitist popinjays get their own balls, drinks, towels and bananas.

Ian Beck
Dearham, Cumbria

SIR – Ladies' final – amazing. Not a single towel moment.

Charles Holden
Lymington, Hampshire

SIR – Having watched Wimbledon with my husband and not getting much conversation from him, I have come to the conclusion that the camera for Centre Court is operated by a man. I say this because all the pictures of the crowd showed amply chested women. Where is the male totty for us downtrodden womenfolk?

A.K.
London SE22

SIR — I continue to be impressed with the Wimbledon authorities' scheduling. When Andy Murray won his first round match, I had just enough time to prepare the drink which my wife demands at exactly 6p.m. each evening.

Brian D. Hamilton
Ponteland, Northumberland

SIR — I am not a pop star, fading or current, I am not a sportsman who doesn't shave and is covered in tattoos and I am not a film actor or a television presenter. I am a normal hard-working Englishman who does his best for the community and who loves tennis — will I ever get an invitation to the Royal Box?

Ian Franklin
Totnes, Devon

ROYAL BLUSHES

IT'S A (FEMALE) PRINCESS

SIR — The august *Irish Times* reported online yesterday: 'It's a girl: Kate Middleton gives birth to a daughter' — a hurried alteration to their earlier headline: 'Kate Middleton gives birth to a daughter; it's a girl'.

Paddy (I'm a man) McGarvey
Cambridge

SIR — We were in France and a message came saying that the new baby was called Charlotte Elizabeth Diana Sue. We spent several minutes discussing where the Sue came from, until we remembered it was the name of our babysitter.

Jane Rice-Oxley
Denmead, Hampshire

SIR — Surprisingly, I seem to be the only person who has noticed that Princess Charlotte's first Christian name contains all the letters of Carole, her maternal grandmother.

Stephanie Crabtree
Scarborough, North Yorkshire

SIR – When Prince William married Ms Middleton, the comparisons made implied that he was marrying his mother. Now, according to the nauseating drivel on your front page this morning, he seems to have fathered his mother. This is beyond Oedipus.

Jane Bonner
Pudsey, West Yorkshire

ROYAL CHILDLINE

SIR – Prince William needs to take care: after a couple of years watching Aston Villa, Prince George might decide to report him to ChildLine.

Kevin Platt
Walsall, West Midlands

SIR – What if Prince George wants to be a ballet dancer?

Pamela Plumb
London NW1

SIR – On hearing Prince William refer to the Duchess as 'the missus' my wife turned to me and said, 'If you ever call me that you're out.'

John Gibson
Standlake, Oxfordshire

KING ANDREW I

SIR – Apropos the scandal surrounding the Duke of York, could we not send him north to be king of a newly independent Scotland? This would solve two problems for England.

Peter Heap
Manuden, Essex

SIR – Perhaps Prince Andrew and the American lady levelling sexual accusations against him should appear on *The Jeremy Kyle Show*. She could tearfully explain her grievances and he could enter as the pantomime villain to be booed and hissed by the audience, while Mr Kyle berated him loudly, as is his way.

Both could then be made to take a lie-detector test and, in time-honoured fashion, stalk off the stage if they disagreed with its findings.

Of course, nothing would be concluded but it would all be great fun.

Ted Shorter
Tonbridge, Kent

SIR – Prince Andrew has emphasised in Davos that he wants to 'concentrate on his work' rather than the speculation about his private life.

Can anyone clarify what his work is and who he is representing at the Davos forum?

Maurice Hastings
Bickington, Devon

SIR – I notice that after recent events Randy Andy is keeping his head down, so to speak.

Jeremy Nicholas
Great Bardfield, Essex

SIR – It would be a pity if the throwing of snowballs were to be outlawed. I lobbed a snowball at Prince Andrew in the West Stand at Twickenham at the Varsity Match in 1981. It missed him.

Jeremy Latham
Winchester

SIR – Why was Prince Andrew dressed in a suit on the balcony of Buckingham Palace?

Are there no regiments left for him to be in charge of?

Leslie Watson
Swansea

COMPANION OF NO HONOUR

SIR – For the umpteenth time in our 46-year marriage, my wife has systematically read through all the Honours awarded on the Queen's Official Birthday. Today she commented that after all that time we seem to be the only people in the UK without an Honour. How can this be?

Lawrence Gordon
Sutton Coldfield, West Midlands

JAWOHL, MEINE KÖNIGIN

SIR – Had the *Sun* photographers been around on the streets of Bermondsey in the early days of the Blitz, when we were being bombed nightly, they could have seen scores of us kids climbing over bomb sites, emerging to give the Nazi salute, then the Goose step, then a gesture involving two fingers and finally an English four-letter word in place of *Heil* before the word Hitler.

No doubt the gutter press of the day could have published a picture headlined: 'Working class children support the Nazis'. Things are rarely what they seem.

Our Queen cannot respond personally but perhaps she may like to join 95 per cent of the population in giving a similar two-fingered salute to the *Sun*.

Patrick Sullivan
Godalming, Surrey

SIR — My best friend and I, aged about seven years in the early 1940s, used to act the part of a saluting German and a Briton, before engaging in friendly punching and wrestling.

We had also drawn up a plan to go into hiding on a hillside should the Germans invade our lovely Shropshire and roll logs down the hill in order to derail the Coalport Dodger steam train if it carried any Germans.

Ron Kirby
Dorchester, Dorset

SIR — Can I hand myself in to the authorities? In 1941, or thereabouts, I learned the phrase 'Ich dien mein Führer', just in case the Nazis invaded. I don't suppose the fact that I was ten years old would make any difference.

A.B.
Bristol

SIR — How do we know they weren't having dog training lessons? The royals are well known for their love of dogs; maybe the Queen Mother was showing her daughters how to tell a dog to stop and stay.

Georgie Helyer
Hanging Langford, Wiltshire

SIR — What a lot of stuff and nonsense. It was an extraordinary salute, as was goose stepping — but what fun to copy! My parents were sailing off Helgoland in the mid-1930s when a day excursion boat from the German mainland came by.

All the tourists crowded to look at this little sailing ship, giving quite a list to their vessel. My father turned to my mother and said, 'Let's have some fun.'

They did the Nazi salute and without exception everyone on the tourist boat responded.

(This needs a cartoonist to illustrate the full glory of the event.)

Astrid Llewellyn
Playford, Suffolk

SIR — Hitler's Nazis hijacked the straight arm salute in much the same way the British National Party tried to hijack the flag of St George.

In the 1960s in Austria I witnessed a class of teenagers with their instructor return from an afternoon's skiing. Having removed their skis they all turned towards the mountain, raised their right arm in salute and cried 'Heil Berg'. Nobody turned a hair.

Jonathan Goodall
Bath

WHEN GERRY MET CHARLES

SIR – I applaud Prince Charles for agreeing to talk with a former member of the IRA. However, that does not give Mr Adams the right to call him Charles.

P.B.
Hitchin, Hertfordshire

SIR – The shaking of hands between Prince Charles and Gerry Adams has been described as historic. How will the shaking of hands, should it ever happen, between Prince Charles and the BBC's Nicholas Witchell be viewed?

David Howarth
Bromley Cross, Lancashire

SIR – One wonders what the benchmark for success is with the meeting between Gerry Adams and Prince Charles. Perhaps that Adams starts writing green spider letters and HRH grows a beard?

Keith Flett
London N17

BRAVO, PRINCE CHARLES

SIR – A brief perusal of Prince Charles's letters is very difficult to evince any reaction other than 'Bravo'.

Charles Pugh
London SW10

SIR – Prince Charles is entitled to his views. However, with the exception of his knowledge about being a prince, his views are no more authoritative than anyone else who takes an interest in a particular subject. In fact, in most cases they may be less authoritative, since he has never worked, for example, in the health service or seen active military service or been trained as an architect or town planner.

So why doesn't he do what the rest of us do with varied success: write to the Letters page of *The Daily Telegraph*?

Charles Essex
Leamington Spa, Warwickshire

DEAR DAILY
TELEGRAPH

LONG-DISTANCE
RELATIONSHIP

SIR – I have previously enjoyed a close relationship
with the *Telegraph*, but since your move to a large
font, I find that I have to keep it at arm's-length.
Perhaps abandoned and confiscated selfie sticks
could be repurposed as *Telegraph* distancing
devices.

Richard Weeks
Felixstowe, Suffolk

SIR – You have clearly spent several hundred
pounds to give some school-leaver a free hand to
redesign our newspaper.

Your charitable gesture has robbed the paper of
its serious and adult presence and turned it into the
worst form of what once would have been called a
girly look comic.

Using coloured type that can't be read in artificial
light and employing gimmick fonts that have no
presence, let alone body, you have succeeded in
proving the truth behind that old American dictum:
'If it ain't broke, don't fix it'.

Arthur W.J.G. Ord-Hume
Guildford, Surrey

SIR – The Austin News typeface with wider spacing
might help those readers who need to chase each

line with their index finger while reading, but for the rest of us it's just an ugly change.

Andrew Luff
London NW1

SIR — Was it the intention of those who designed the new format *Telegraph* to contribute to marital disharmony? At breakfast my wife and I tackle the crossword together, then at coffee time we can concentrate on our favourite bits — she to the puzzles page, I to the letters.

What do we find now? The puzzles and letter sections are back-to-back on the same sheet.

It really is too much to bear, especially as my wife always wins the ensuing verbal tug-of-war. Please, if you can, rescue me from this terrible situation.

Roy Ellis
Shrewsbury

CROSS WORDS

SIR — My wife always says that when we do the cryptic crossword together at lunchtime it is our 'togetherness time'. She regularly sends off the weekend prize crosswords.

However, when a handsome fountain pen, Biro and notebook came through the post this week the 'togetherness' went out of the window. She has become quite big-headed.

George Howard
Melbourn, Cambridgeshire

SIR – My husband's mood was by no means enhanced this morning by being asked to provide Beyoncé's maiden name in answer to one of the clues: even my offer to purchase a year's subscription to one of the 'celebrity' magazines for future reference purposes didn't exactly help.

Judith A. Scott
St Ives, Cambridgeshire

PUSHING DOWN THE DAISIES

SIR – Am I alone in thinking that more and more people appear to shun traditional funeral flowers? For example, in your July 9 edition there were 20 death notices. Eight specifically requested that there be no flowers, three requested donations and six requested family flowers only.

Continuing this theme, I have added a codicil to my will: if nobody has given me flowers in my lifetime, I certainly do not require them when I'm dead.

Charles Holcombe
Brighton

SIR – A recent article informed us that the baby boomer generation are becoming more creative in their plans for their funeral services. I intend to have 'The Wheels on the Bus' played at the end of mine. That should create a stir.

Michael Cattell
Mollington, Cheshire

SIR – One has heard of strange coincidences but this must be a record: under Births on May 6 was an announcement of the birth of a young man to be named Rafferty Rocket. My Springer/Collie cross is called Rafferty and his best friend is a Lurcher called Rocket.

They are an engaging couple and if young Rafferty Rocket Trentham would like to see a photograph of them, his parents are more than welcome to get in touch.

Susan Fulford-Dobson
Rotherfield Greys, Oxfordshire

VICTIMISED READERS

SIR – Every morning, as I sip tea in bed while reading the *Telegraph*, I become a victim of Flying Page Syndrome.

Instead of turning over a double page which remains firmly anchored by the thumb of my right hand, a casually flipped rogue singleton will fly off the bed and on to the floor.

May I appeal for one extra page of your splendid paper to obviate this nuisance?

Geraldine Durrant
East Grinstead, West Sussex

SIR – Since I've taken to reading *The Daily Telegraph* on my Kindle I note that, when I close my eyes tightly, I no longer see swirling paisley patterns but images of text. Should I be concerned?

Chris Lee
Berkhamsted, Hertfordshire

BREASTS ARE BEST

SIR – Your paper contained an article by Bryony Gordon posing the question: 'Can it be that breasts are going out of fashion?'

Has Bryony completely lost touch with reality? Does she inhabit a parallel universe? I spent some time yesterday conducting a straw poll of 100 million men worldwide, a reasonable sample I think you will agree, and 100 per cent of those polled disagreed profoundly with the suggestion.

Philip Thomas
Arundel, West Sussex

DEAR PICTURE EDITOR

SIR – It would be most appreciated if you would be kind enough not to publish photographs of Nicola Sturgeon in my morning paper; it spoils my breakfast.

Bernard George
Hadleigh, Essex

SIR – I'm confused. Your article 'Caravanning just got a Glam-Over' includes a photograph of Coleen Rooney which informs us that she has recently purchased a caravan. Does this mean that I should or should not purchase said item?

Richard J.C. English
King's Lynn, Norfolk

SIR – Your publication of the extraordinary picture of a totally naked Helena Bonham Carter apparently pleasuring a dead tuna in an attempt to draw attention to overfishing around Britain may bring about repercussions from other worthy organisations.

Among others, I hear the Donkey Sanctuary is always in desperate need of money and publicity.

Lance Warrington
Northleach, Gloucestershire

SIR — It was very interesting to read in Letters to the Editor about Field Marshal Montgomery possibly having Asperger's. What a pity, however, that the picture was printed the wrong way round. As my husband Philip pointed out, you never had a right-hand drive Jeep, his beret is tilted the wrong way and his badge is on the wrong side.

Do better next time, Pike!

Janet Berridge
Oakham, Rutland

SIR — Your newspaper should know better than to stereotype public-school boys. The Wall Game photo indeed depicts Etonians in one of the more bizarre activities enjoyed by very few at that establishment. Your picture of the two 'toffs' being observed by the three 'scruffs' is, however, of boys from that lesser school in Harrow. I know because one is my father-in-law.

Ben Blower
Ringsfield, Suffolk

USUAL SUSPECTS

SIR — What a great selection of names in the letters page today: Prof Pheby, Jane Jacklin, Damien McCrystal, G.G. Garner, Jackie McCrindle, Christo Scaramanga and Leslie V. Snow. Sounds like the chief suspects in an episode of *Midsomer Murders*.

> **Jo Marchington**
> Ashtead, Surrey

SIR – I see that Jane O'Nions of Sevenoaks is back from holiday.

> **Brian Keeling**
> Denmead, Hampshire

SIR – Nepotism. Elitism. Favouritism. Bias. Snobbery. The criteria for getting anything published in the *Telegraph* are crystal clear. Would you like a couple of twee lines about jam? Or will any rubbish do as long as it's sent in by a doctor of something or anyone else you think worth sucking up to?

Your birthdays list shows what a load of creeps you are. Who the hell cares if so-and-so headmaster (obviously your ex-headmaster) or judge is 80 today?

> **S.B.**
> Portsmouth (is that too rough for your
> sensibilities?), Hampshire

SIR – Your lead letter today regarding the Queen's Speech being too timid on matters of constitutional reform is signed by Revd Andrew McLuskey of Stanwell, Middlesex.

Could this be the same Revd Andrew McLuskey whose letter on the same topic appears in today's *Times* letters page, word for word?

Oddly, the latter letter gives the vicar's address as 'Staines, Surrey'. How often do repeats like this happen?

T. Edward Bevin
St Albans, Hertfordshire

SIR – I have noticed an increased number of letters from Stratford-upon-Avon. Does this mean that it has displaced Tunbridge Wells as the 'Disgusted' centre of dissent?

Philip Brennan
Oxhill, Warwickshire

SIR – I was delighted to hear from my son that he has started to read the *Telegraph*. Less impressed, however, to discover in one of your letters book that this was because his wife liked a broadsheet for the bottom of the parrots' cage.

Amanda Howard
Enfield, Middlesex

SIR – Some years ago, prior to publication of your first volume of unpublished letters, *Am I Alone In Thinking . . .?*, I received an email from you asking if I had any objection to a letter of mine being included.

I replied that I had no objection and eagerly awaited publication.

Imagine my disappointment when I discovered that my letter had not been included.

Also, I have not appeared in any subsequent volume.

Is this the ultimate put-down?

Dennis Waterman
Ashburton, Devon

GOODBYE AND GOOD LUCK

SIR – I have just had a letter asking me to renew my subscription to your paper. Can I make it conditional on eliminating any mention of George Clooney for at least a week or two? While no doubt he is quite a decent fellow I fail to see what qualification he has to appear in nearly every edition of your paper for the last 12 months.

It's getting beyond a joke.

Sid Davies
Bramhall, Cheshire

SIR – I have been taking *The Daily Telegraph* for 43 years on the premise that I was reading a serious centre-right newspaper. Today's front page was the last straw.

The lead article, featuring yet another health

scare story, no doubt copy and pasted by an intern, is totally irrelevant. The silly young lady with the suitably pained expression could well wonder if the whistlers were doing so out of sympathy. Then came trivia about banks and holidays and finally a piece of news (Nepal) and the genius that is Matt.

Oh, and I nearly forgot, the daily extract from the Tory press release (no doubt copy and pasted).

I doubt that you will print this in the paper, but I'm sure Mr Hollingsworth [sic] might put it in his end-of-season book.

Good bye.

John Newman
Pattishall, Northamptonshire

MATT AND ALEX ARE AWAY

SIR – In future could you please make sure that Matt and Alex don't both book holiday at the same time.

Have you any idea what it's like to sit down for breakfast and not be able to start my day with a smile?

David Tinton
Stow-on-the-Wold, Gloucestershire

P.S.

SPECIAL DELIVERY

SIR – Shortly after our marriage, in 1971, we received a letter from my wife's friend. It was addressed thus:

> *Barry and Liz (Evans?)*
> *White Cottage by the stream*
> *With black and white spotty dog*
> *New Inn*
> *Pontypool*

It arrived the day after posting. Top marks to the post office, especially when you consider that our surname is Davies.

Barry and Liz Davies
Rogerstone, Gwent

RIP, CILLA

SIR – The death of Cilla Black is very sad news. However, what I find equally sad is that it takes the death of one of our legends for the public to be reminded of their talents.

It would have been nice for Cilla to have heard her songs played more frequently in recent years – and to have heard the media speak so well of her while she was still alive.

I wonder how many older stars miss the adoration and warmth, and feel lonely and rejected.

R. Allen
Waltham on the Wolds, Leicestershire

RIP, CECIL

SIR — The sorry story of how a trophy hunter killed Cecil, Zimbabwe's favourite lion, using a bow and arrow reminds me of an American big game hunter who claimed, long ago, to have hunted lions with a spear.

When I remarked that this sounded extremely dangerous he replied, 'Not really. A friend of mine used to hunt lions with a club — mind you, there were over 200 members in his club.'

Andrew M. Courtney
Hampton Wick, Middlesex

SIR — Perhaps Walter Palmer, the American dentist who killed Cecil, could be persuaded to take his bow and arrow elsewhere. Some years ago there were rumours that Barbary lions, long thought extinct, had survived in northern Syria.

Richard Lowe
Horsham, West Sussex

SIR – Maybe Walter Palmer could be prevailed upon to come to this country and shoot seagulls instead of lions.

Margaret Wilkinson
Sixpenny Handley, Dorset

SIR – Am I alone in thinking that much less fuss and furore would have been caused if the American dentist had shot Sepp Blatter instead?

Peter Thompson
Sutton, Surrey